PETER CHAY

SABAH

THE LAND BELOW THE WIND

Published by

foto technik sdn bhd

Designed and produced by Peter Chay
Text by Kim Lee and A.G. Sullivan
Edited by Ee Sim Teo-Machado and
Yee Fong Chun

Perpustakaan Negara Malaysia
Cataloquing-in-Publication-Data
Sabah — The Land Below The Wind

ISBN 967-9981-12-6

1. Sabah — Description and Travel
2. Sabah — Social conditions
   915.9521

Colour Separations by: Times Graphic Scanning Sdn. Bhd., Malaysia.
Typesetting by: Tye Cine and Stills Sdn. Bhd., Malaysia.
Printed by: Kim Hup Lee Printing Co Pte Limited, Singapore.

Published by
Foto Technik Sdn. Bhd., No. 116A Jalan Burhanuddin Helmi,
Taman Tun Dr Ismail, 60000 Kuala Lumpur, Malaysia.

First Malaysian Edition
September 1988

Tuan Yang Terutama Yang Di-Pertua Negeri Sabah,
Tan Sri Datuk Haji Mohammad Said Bin Keruak, P.M.N., S.P.D.K.

The publisher is greatly indepted to the Sabah State Government, whose generous support and encouragement helped make the publication of this book possible.

The five guiding principles of the Nation known as the Rukunegara
have been formulated to bring about national unity to the multi-racial
people of Malaysia.

- Belief in God
- Loyalty to King and Country
- Upholding the Constitution
- Rule of Law
- Good Behaviour and Morality

To God be the glory for all that He has done.

Datuk Joseph Pairin Kitingan
Chief Minister of Sabah

Foreword

This beautiful book presents a bird's eye view of Sabah, the eastern-most state of Malaysia. It spotlights the state's towns and villages as well as its many natural wonders, including the crown jewel of Malaysia, the majestic, mysterious Mt. Kinabalu.

Interwoven in this amazing tapestry of northern Borneo are its primeval rain forests, interrupted here and there by farmlands, towns and villages and vast tracts of plantations. Criss-crossed by deep gorges, awesome mountain ranges and placid meanders which feed into the blue, island studded ocean, these lush landscapes of Borneo are undergoing rapid change.

This is a land peopled by many races each with its own cultures and traditions as rich and varied as the natural resources from which the state's population of slightly over a million people draw sustenance.

Agnes Keith who popularised the name "Land Below The Wind" may have also alluded to the "wind of change" which was sweeping through the entire world in the immediate post war period. The fact that Great Britain took over North Borneo from the Chartered Company and made it a Crown Colony in the midst of the decolonising process which was already gathering momentum at the time, must have seemed to many that North Borneo was indeed a land that would never change.

Lying just out of reach of the devastating typhoon, North Borneo slumbered on under the benevolent rule of its colonial masters.

The wind of change did come to Sabah. On 31 August, 1963 Sabah was granted self-rule by Great Britain. 16 days later she joined up with Sarawak, Singapore and the then Federation of Malaya to form Malaysia.

Since then, in a matter of barely 25 years, this former British colony has achieved a metamorphosis that defies even the wildest imagination of those who had last seen it as a sleepy backwater where the people appeared oblivious of the great surge to the 20th Century by countries the world over. At that time the 20th Century seemed destined never to touch Borneo.

This book is a celebration of that historic event 25 years ago. It adds significance to and enhances the Silver Jubilee which Sabah celebrates this year beginning on 16 September, 1988. It documents the stage of development and progress which has been achieved by four successive administrations in the post independence era.

Most important of all this book introduces Sabah to the outside world. Many people in the West have heard of Malaysia. Many have read about the mysterious island called Borneo where headhunters roamed and the "wild men of Borneo" lived on tree-tops. Not many people realise that North Borneo and Sabah are one and the same place. Fewer still can visualise a spectacle of television antennae craning out of the *atap* roofs of many bamboo homes in the depth of Sabah.

This is a land of contrasts. It has the trappings of what the latest of modern civilisation can offer and which money can buy. It has modern buildings, the daily traffic jams, the fast food restaurants. It has vast tracts of commercial plantations supported by the most up-to-date processing mills. But it is also a land where many inhabitants still use ancient implements and techniques inherited from their forebears to eke out a living in the hills far away from modern amenities.

At least this is as things are as we approach the threshold of the 21st Century. No one can foresee what manner of change will take place in the next 25 years, but what we have achieved today is what matters most as we commemorate the last 25 years of our journey since we took the destiny of our country in our own hands.

I hope that this beautiful land and the diversity of people and cultures which Peter Chay has captured on film and presented so skilfully in this book will, through it, be better known and appreciated both at home and abroad.

I congratulate Peter Chay on the successful publication of this book, and I thank him for the hard work and dedication which he has put into this beautiful publication.

Datuk Joseph Pairin Kitingan
Chief Minister of Sabah

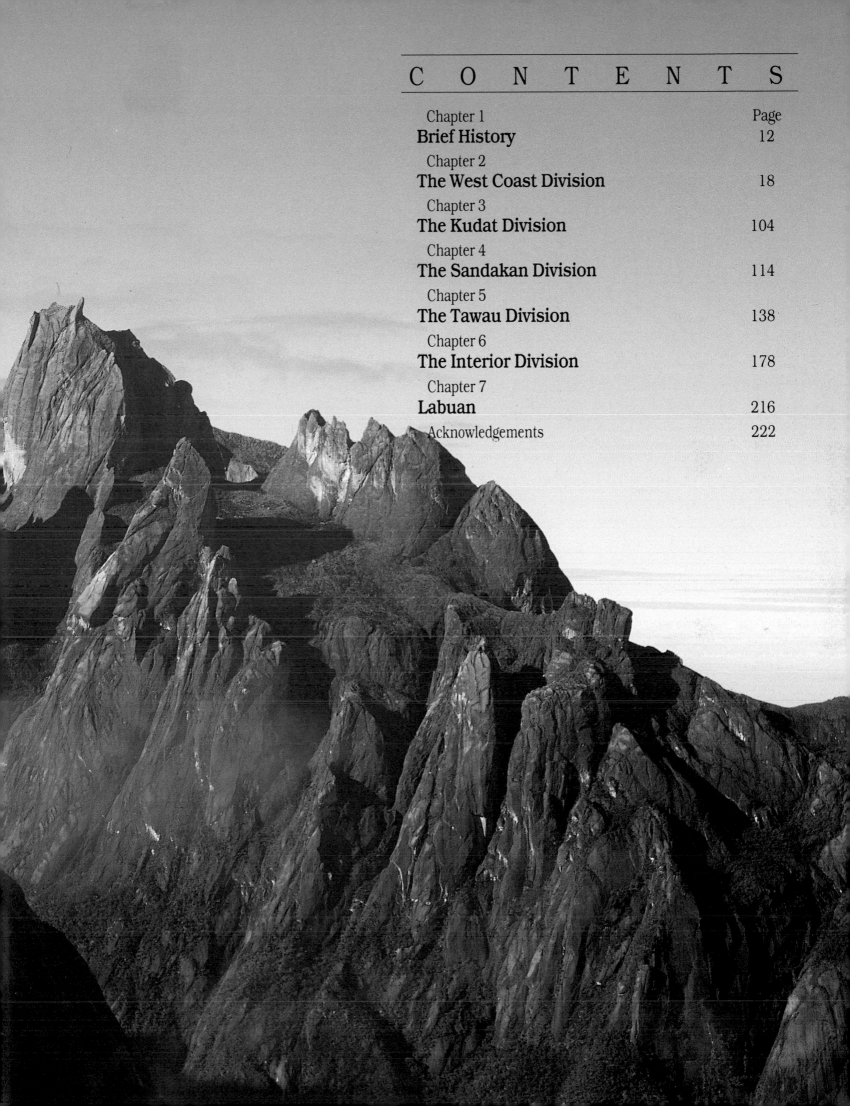

CONTENTS

Chapter One

BRIEF HISTORY

Sabah, 'The Land Below The Wind' – is a lush green state criss-crossed by swift flowing and long meandering rivers and lofty mountain ranges. This East Malaysian State with an area of 73,600 square kilometres, sits on the northern tip of the island of Borneo, encompassed by three seas – the South China, Sulu and Celebes Seas. It is blessed by one grand feature – Mount Kinabalu.

The romantic tag – The Land Below The Wind – was given by seafarers long ago, reflecting Sabah's geographical position, just south of the typhoon belt which blights the Philippines. The tag was later popularized by Agnes Keith, an American lady who lived in Sabah with her husband in the early part of this century. Although Agnes was used to city comforts, she could not help but fall under the spell of Sabah's rustic beauty.

That beauty still exists today. Pristine islands whose waters house some of the world's most beautiful coral gardens, unique flora and fauna, while the many friendly ethnic groups preserve interesting legends of mountains and jungles, of their origins and spirits, colourful cultures, dances, music and intricate handicrafts.

Geologically, Sabah is young. Although our planet dates back 3,500 million years, the rocks that form the island of Borneo are only 200 million years old, while the tropical jungles were formed a mere 10 million years or so ago. The Borneo coastline was formed only about 10,000 years ago after the last of the gigantic blocks of ice from the last Ice Age melted away to raise the levels of the sea.

Before the rising seas defined what is now Borneo, the island was part of Sundaland, a huge land mass that encompassed the Malay Peninsula, and most of what is present day Indonesia and the Philippines. At that time the land stretched from what is now Scotland to Sabah. But the early settlers of Sabah were displaced tribes of mainland Asia – most probably forced out by more advanced or stronger people – who found their way to Borneo either directly across the seas, through the Philippines Islands, or the Malay Peninsula.

Some of the earliest, so far discovered people in Sabah were inhabitants on the shores of Lake Tingkayu. Lake Tingkayu was formed by a lava flow from the now extinct mostyn volcano which blocked the Tingkayu river, forming a lake. Long after the water vanished, beautifully cut stone tools dating back as far as 27,000 years were unearthed there. These artefacts shed some light as to the life of the people. This site is unique in South East Asia as the level of technology associated with the manufacture of stone tools pre-dates anything so far discovered.

When the water left Tingkayu, it uncovered caves at Baturong which were etched out of limestone that had been laid in the sea some 140 million years ago. The caves, forced up by a geological action, became homes to nomadic tribes in the next few thousand years.

Like those at Baturong, the Madai Caves also saw the passing of some of these early people. The floors of the caves recorded the development of these people from the use of stone tools to primitive pottery, bronze and iron.

Chinese trade and diplomatic relations with Borneo were recorded in Chinese annals, as far back as 600 AD. The arrival of the Chinese spawned the development of trade between Borneo and China which is relected in the Sabah Museum, whose ceramics collection dates back to the pre-Sung Dynasty. The demand for Chinese products, particularly ceramic articles such as dragon jars, was strong. These jars and other ceramics became an integral part of local life and were used for burial rituals, dowry gifts as well as for water storage and wine making.

The Chinese traded with the coastal dwellers of Borneo who in turn traded with the peoples of the interior for products such as jungle produce. These include camphor and sandalwood, deer and rhinoceros horn, edible bird's nests and hornbill ivory. The Chinese value the solid casque af a hornbill more than jade.

Not long after the Chinese, traders from nearby Brunei, Malaya, Indonesia and the Philippines also arrived to trade with the locals. The arrival of Europeans in Borneo was first recorded on July 17, 1521 when the Spanish fleet under Magellen sailed up the Brunei river. On leaving Brunei, they stopped at either Balambangan Island or Banggi Island to repair their vessels.

Meanwhile, the British were becoming more aware of the vast trade potential in the Far East and vied with the Dutch and Portuguese for a share. The British, eager to expand their influence further in South-East Asia, set up a trading station under the East India Company on Balambangan Island in 1773. But due to mismanagement and insults to Suluk Datu' by the company's representative John Herbert, the site was overrun by Suluk pirates on March 5, 1775. The settlement was re-established in 1805 only to be abandoned again in the same year by orders from London. It was a bad decision to make Balambangan Island a trading port. It was a bad site, disease ridden, short of water and had a very shallow harbour causing ships to drop anchor at least 500 metres from the shore.

Despite Sabah's reputation as a haunt for pirates, home to headhunters and rife with tropical diseases, there was no holding back the Europeans. Steadily, they began to extend their influence over South-East Asia.

The Dutch, having gained control over the greater part of Borneo, became interested in the north. The British, the Portuguese and the Americans were also interested in Sabah. Even the Italians in 1870 conceived the plan of establishing a penal colony on Balambangan Island. Northern Borneo was perhaps the last piece of available land in the area and thus competition was strong.

In 1850 the United States of America had negotiated a commercial treaty with the Sultan of Brunei. This treaty had been forgotten until in 1864 when President Lincoln appointed C. Lee Moses as the American Consul to Brunei. He arrived in Brunei in July 1865. Moses quickly succeeded in persuading the Sultan to cede a large tract of land to the north to him for a period of ten years in return for certain payments. But it appeared that Moses was more interested in lining his own pocket than representing his country for no sooner had he received the cessions then he went off to Hong Kong and sold them. The purchasers, Americans Joseph W. Torrey and Thomas B. Harris, set up a Colony at the mouth of the Kimanis River and called it Ellena. But the colony was badly managed. Disease, death and desertion by the immigrant labourers led to the collapse of Ellena towards the end of 1866. The only visible sign now remaining of the American Trading Company is the tombstone of Thomas B. Harris.

In January 1875, Baron Von Overbeck, the Austrian Consul at Hong Kong acquired the rights of the American Trading Company from Torrey. After failing to interest the Austrian Government who were at this time still without any 'colonies', he turned to Alfred Dent in London who showed great interest. With Dent's money in hand, Overbeck returned to Labuan. He secured a new treaty with the Sultan of Brunei on December 29, 1877 and proceeded to Jolo where he secured a similar treaty from the Sultan of Sulu on January 22, 1878. Overbeck sold out to Dent in 1880.

In July 1881, Alfred Dent and his brother formed the British North Borneo Provisional Association and transferred their deeds for the sum of £120,000. It later became the British North Borneo Company and received a Royal Charter on November 1, 1881. The land was opened for development by the British Company and eventually became a British Protectorate in 1888, thus sealing it against occupation by other foreign powers.

The foundations was thus laid for economic growth in North Borneo. The company restored peace to the land where piracy and tribal feuds had grown rampant. It abolished slavery and set up transport, health and education services for the people. Chinese immigrants were wooed to boost the small population of less than 100,000 so that labour and capital could be obtained for development of the land. The combined effort of the locals and immigrants coaxed order out of the jungle land. Very soon, towns, a small timber industry, tobacco and rubber plantations began to thrive.

Despite two major rebellions against British insensitivity to local customs and feelings, the company fared very well in bringing progress to North Borneo. It must be remembered, however, the Company's primary responsibility remained to its shareholders, it was in business to make a profit. However, World War Two brought an abrupt halt to that prosperous existence with the Japanese Army invasion on New Year's Day, 1942. With the aim af a "Greater East Asia" Japanese troops occupied Labuan followed by Beaufort, Jesselton (now Kota Kinabalu) and Sandakan. The meagre North Borneo Armed Constabulary with only 650 men, and the Volunteer Forces hardly provided any resistance to slow down the Japanese invasion.

The Europeans were interned, public services ceased to exist and there was widespread poverty, disease and malnutrition.

Liberation came in June 1945 when the Australian Ninth Division began to retake Sabah from the Japanese Army. What they saw when they entered the major towns was total devastation. The towns had been razed to the ground by allied bombing. Martial law was declared and order slowly returned.

The British North Borneo Company could not afford to rebuild the territory after the devastation of the war and decided to sell its interests to the British Government. On July 15, 1946 the British Protectorate of North Borneo became a Crown Colony. As a result of this change in status, North Borneo had access to British Government funds for reconstruction.

Under colonial rule, much of the Chartered Company's system of administration – the Residency and District structure started by the first governor, Sir William Hood Treacher and William Pryer – was retained. Initially, there were only two Residencies – the East Coast and

West Coast – with their headquarters at Sandakan and Jesselton respectively.

Each Residency was divided into Provinces, later known as Districts, which were run by District Officers. By 1922, there were five Residencies to accomodate new areas opened up for development. These were the West Coast, Kudat, Tawau, Interior and East Coast Residencies. These Residencies were in turn divided into 17 Districts.

Under the Residency and District System, the British held top posts while native chiefs managed the people at grassroots level. This, however, was not a conscious attempt by the British to instill indirect rule but a convenient arrangement for the District Officers who were unfamiliar with local customs.

After World War Two, the British Military Administration administered the state until July 15, 1946, when civil government resumed. A Governor and Commander-in-Chief was appointed to administer the colony of North Borneo with the assistance of an Advisory Council consisting of three ex-officio members – the Chief Secretary, the Attorney-General and the Financial Secretary – together with other members both official and unofficial whom the Governor choose to appoint.

In 1950 the Advisory Council was replaced by the Executive and Legislative Councils. The Executive Council functioned as a form of 'Cabinet' headed by the Chief Secretary and in addition to the Attorney General and the Financial Secretary comprised two officials and four nominated members. The Governor presided at the Executive Council meetings and he alone was entitled to submit questions to the Council.

The Legislative Council consisted of the Governor as President, the usual three ex-officio members, nine official members and ten nominated members. The Legislative Council was the law making body.

The day-to-day running of the state was handled by a number of departments, some of which were revamped under colonial rule. The Agriculture Department, for instance, broke away from the Forest Department while the Posts Department was merged with the Telegraph Department. In addition, a separate Department of Civil Aviation was set up.

The high-ranking administrative posts were held by British officers and it took some time before local officers began to take on more responsible jobs. In fact, it was only in 1957 that the first Sabahan filled an administrative officer's post.

By the early 1960s, many locals were already involved in the day-to-day running of their own land which was then preparing to join the Federation of Malaysia as an independent member state. The British name of "North Borneo" was dropped and the original name "Sabah" re-instated.

The idea of a Federation of Malaysia was proposed in May 1961 by Tunku Abdul Rahman, the first Prime Minister of Malaya and later the first Prime Minister of Malaysia. The Tunku believed that unity and understanding between Malaya, Sabah, Sarawak, Singapore and Brunei would contribute to peace and stability in South-East Asia.

Initially, the proposed Federation was rejected by the three states of Borneo. But the rejection did serve a purpose – it stirred the first patriotic feelings in Sabah and sparked off the growth of local political parties.

The first local political party was formed by a timber magnate and newspaper publisher, Donald Stephens, in August 1961. It was called the United National Kadazan Organization (UNKO). Five months later, the United Sabah National Organization (USNO), headed by Datu Mustapha Harun, came into being. In January 1962, a third native party – the United National Pasok Momogun Organization (Pasok Momogun) – was set up. Political parties from the smaller Chinese and Indian communities also emerged.

During this period, various views on whether or not Sabah should join the proposed Federation of Malaysia were expressed by these parties, but one common sentiment was that they were worried at being dominated by the more advanced and better educated people of Malaya. They felt that unless there were safeguards, Sabah might be swamped by people from Malaya who would take over senior positions. Religion and language were also dominant issues that demanded attention.

In the first direct elections for District and Town Councils, the Sabah Alliance Party – comprising UNKO, USNO and SCA (Sabah Chinese Association) – was voted to power. They later formed a united front for Sabahs entry into Malaysia.

The proposed Federation of Malaysia was not only opposed by some quarters in the states concerned, but also by the governments of Indonesia and the Philippines. To ease the tension, the United Nations sent a mission to Sabah and Sarawak to check on the opinions of the people. Their report on September 14, 1963, said that majority of the people in the two states wanted to be part of the Federation. Two days later, the Federation of Malaysia came into being.

The governments of Indonesia and the Philippines refused to recognize the Federation and "Confrontation" developed between Indonesia and Malaysia. Diplomatic relations were severed and British and Malaysian troops formed defences along the Sabah-Kalimantan border areas.

The tide, however, began to turn on June 3, 1966 when the Philippines agreed to come to terms with Malaysia.

The following month, Malaysia and Indonesia cleared the air with a peace treaty.

Sabah's short history since independence was marked by some political upheavals. There were struggles between individuals and component parties of the Sabah Alliance. The first state general elections in April 1967 saw USNO emerge as the dominant party with Tun Datu Mustapha Harun becoming the Chief Minister. But political infighting did not stop. Disillusioned, the people shifted loyalty to the newly-formed multi-racial Bersatu Rakyat Jelata Sabah (Berjaya) which came to power in the 1976 state elections. Tun Fuad Stephens became the Chief Minister.

The Berjaya victory in 1976 ushered a return to more democratic rule. Berjaya continued to rule until 1985, but there was increasingly public dissatisfaction with the party which was then under the leadership of Datuk Harris Salleh.

Datuk Joseph Pairin Kitingan left Berjaya to form a new multi-racial party, Parti Bersatu Sabah (Sabah United Party) or PBS. He became the new Chief Minister when PBS emerged victorious in the 1985 polls. In fresh elections in 1986, the PBS was returned to power with a larger majority in the State Legislative Assembly.

In spite of all the political turbulence, Sabah has been considerable progress, thanks to a series of development plans implemented by both the State and Federal governments. As a result of these concerted efforts, there has been a marked improvement in transportation and other communications, public utilities, housing and social services. In addition, the state's economy has also expanded with timber, crude oil, palm oil, cocoa, copper and rubber becoming the leading export commodities.

Balanced against the rapid development, Sabah's rich natural environment has also been given due recognition and is deservedly receiving protection. One hopes this will ensure that its natural beauty will be preserved for posterity.

While this book is intended as a window to this enthralling land, it cannot adequately impart the nip in a mountain breeze, the warm embrace of transparent waters, the lilting contentment that could set your spirits soaring above valley fields, nor the friendliness of Sabahans who are as wonderfully varied as the scenic contrasts of the land. Altogether, depending on the criteria used, there are about 40 ethnic groups living harmoniously in this richly endowed land. Over 50 languages and approximately 90 dialects are spoken.

The origins of the ethnic groups are charmingly "explained" in an old folk tale that originates in legend and history and is a legacy from Sabah's oldest people. The tale speaks of a place called Nunuk Ragang, the original Sabahan's Garden of Eden, somewhere in the heart of Sabah. A river ran through it with a nunuk or banyan tree on its bank. The native children loved to play in the river and climb the huge branches of the banyan tree to sun themselves – which is how true Sabahans got the golden glow of their skins. People lived happily together and multiplied. Very soon, Nunuk Ragang got too crowded. Families had to move out in search of new places to live. Some came across valley plains and settled there as farmers. Others made their way up the highlands and learned to hunt and reap the bounty of the jungles. Some trekked as far as the sea coast and settled there too. And that was how the people spread across the land.

Many of the ethnic groups share a similar oral history, languages and traditions. However, lack of communication between the people due to the rugged terrain has resulted in the evolution of many dialects in common languages, different dress styles, handicrafts and cultures.

For simplicity, Sabah's major ethnic groupings can be categorised as Kadazans or Dusuns, Bajau, Murut and Chinese sub-groups within these broad classifications.

The Kadazans or Dusuns are the largest grouping forming about one third of the state's population. The name "Kadazan" is relatively new and was created to unite a number of kindred groups mainly along the west coast area.

The Kadazan or Dusun peoples are of the same stock, some preferring to call themselves Dusun, while others retain tribal names such as Rungus, Lotud, Kwijau, etc. Originally the Kadazan or Dusun peoples were farmers although now many have migrated to urban centres and are prominent in the civil service and the professions.

The Muruts (literally meaning 'hill people') inhabit the southern interior area. They were once feared headhunters. Most of the Muruts live in three districts, Tenom, Keningau and Pensiangan where they are mainly longhouse dwellers. Besides hunting with blowpipe and spear, they also gather jungle produce such as rattan and resin as well as plant paddy on a shifting cultivation basis for their livelihood. Old tribal names such as Timogun, Tagol, Nabang, etc are still used to refer to different Murut groups.

Despite their conversion to Christianity and Islam, many of the Kadazan or Dusuns and the Muruts still have ritual specialists to perform certain ceremonies.

The Bajaus are Sabah's second largest indigenous group and can be broadly classified into two – West Coast Bajau and East Coast Bajau. They are found in concentrated numbers on the coastal areas especially from Kota Kinabalu to Kota Belud and around the Semporna area. Originally they were seafarers and at one time many were feared pirates. The West Coast Bajau are now mainly farmers and cattle breeders, the renowned 'cowboy horsemen' of Sabah. The Bajau of the East Coast are traditionally coastal dwellers and fishermen although many have now settled on land. They now form two distinct language groups but still retain tribal names such as Samah and Simanul. The Iranun comprise a kindred group.

The Chinese are the largest non-native group in Sabah. Although some arrived in Sabah more than a thousand years ago, they did not migrate in appreciable numbers until the British North Borneo Company wooed them to stay in the 1880s. Many returned home disillusioned while those who stayed worked in the tobacco plantations, mines and market gardens. Many of them later became shopkeepers and open other business. However, even up to the 1970 census more than 50% of the Chinese were classified as rural and not urban dwellers.

Besides the four major ethnic group already mentioned, Sabah's 1.3 million population also include Suluks, Malays, Idahans, Orang Sungai, Bisaya, Kedayan, Tambanuo, Lotud, Rungus, Buludupis, Tidong and many others, with a sprinkling of Indian, Japanese, Thai, Arab and European origins.

In Sabah, language divisions cut across the accepted ethnic divisions. Names also not a true indication of an individual's ethnic group or his religion. A Chinese name may only reflect distant Chinese ancestry. Ethnically, culturally and religiously, the situation in Sabah is quite bewildering as to make it unique.

(previous pages 8 & 9) A bird's eye view of Mt. Kinabalu West.

(previous pages 10 & 11) A bird's eye view of Mt. Kinabalu East.

The motif is photographed from the Kain Ampik which is used by the Bajaus and other indigenous (Kadazan/Dusun) people of Sabah for decoration in the house during certain function and worn as a headdress as part of the costumes by the Bajaus. It is made by the Iranum of Kota Belud using the backstrap loom.

17

Chapter Two

THE WEST COAST DIVISION

Sunrise on Sabah's West Coast brings yet another day of contrast. The early light that dissolves the damp night air over paddy fields also glints off the glass facade of the imposing 31-storey Sabah Foundation Building. The same light that reaches down turquoise waters to diamond-like fish warms yet another day of commercial bustle in the state capital of Kota Kinabalu.

Already the fish market is in full swing. The catch has been sorted and the first customers are strolling in. Soon the city will catch up, opening the doors of its shopping centres and offices. At Kota Kinabalu's premier beach resort, guests study the breakfast buffet.

Kota Kinabalu, previously Jesselton, is the nerve centre of the state. Administration issues from air-conditioned government offices where the outpost trading station of Jesselton once stood. Its natural, sheltered harbour helped to make Kota Kinabalu the port it is. Today, Government

officials no longer do their rounds of the countryside on horseback along bridle-paths. Instead, they use land cruisers and, if necessary fly, usually by helicopters and light aircraft.

Kota Kinabalu harbour is only one of many on the state's 1,440-kilometre long coast. The Chinese recognised the potential of these anchorages when they started sailing to Sabah and probably set up convenient trading posts along the coast. Fragments of Sung pottery at Abai, near Kota Belud, testify to their presence about a thousand years ago.

Situated close to Kota Kinabalu are Kimanis and Gaya. The former was the first and only American colony while the latter was an outpost trading station set up by the British in 1881. The Gaya station, on Pulau Gaya Island, had good anchorage but its short separation over water made it difficult to administer the West Coast. After the settlement was looted and burnt by rebel and local hero, Mat Salleh, in 1897, Gaya was abandoned for Jesselton.

For years, young Sabahans had been taught to believe that Mat Salleh was a rabble-rouser, a threat to the peace and prosperity that the British had so carefully wrought. But since independence Mat Salleh is seen as a hero, fighting against injustices.

Mat Salleh, the son of a Sulu chief and a Bajau mother, was a trader when the authorities first noticed him in 1894 after his followers had killed two Iban men. Even then, he was a charismatic leader. He was said to have a keen military mind and legend has it that he also had supernatural powers. Whichever the case, he caused a great deal of grief to the British with his raids. People were killed on both sides, yet his band grew whenever he needed followers.

He built several forts in Sabah, sturdy masterpieces that frustrated attempts to catch him. If he felt that the forts were not safe enough, he would melt into the jungle and simply re-appear in another part of the state. The authorities hunted him for years across the wild and a price was put on his capture. He was finally cornered in 1900 at his Tambunan fort and killed by a stray shot in the head.

The West Coast also has its share of war intrigue. The Double Tenth uprising was a bold guerilla movement led by Albert Kwok against the Japanese. Kwok, born in Kuching, Sarawak, had studied in China before arriving in Sabah in 1940, a step ahead of World War Two.

Sabah had suffered terribly under the year-and-a-half of Japanese oppression when Kwok rallied the people against them. He had tried earlier to reach other resistance leaders and the Allied forces but to no avail. Secret meetings were held to gather arms, food and people for the rebellion. Except for a few who had served in the country's Volunteer Force before the war, the people who came forward had no military experience at all. They were a mixed group – Chinese, Suluks, Bajaus and Dusuns.

The attack was planned for October 9, 1943. The resistance fighters, especially the Chinese, hoped to regain freedom the next day, October 10 (10/10), which is also the date of the Chinese National Day. They struck at night at Tuaran, Menggatal and Jesselton. Through their spies, the Japanese knew of the imminent rebellion but never expected the sudden attack. By midnight, fifty Japanese were already dead.

The guerillas went on to hit Kota Belud on October 11. But by then, they had begun to run low on ammunition and food. The Japanese recovered swiftly and an aggressive manhunt was mounted for the rebels on October 13. The guerillas and their supporters were picked up across Sabah over the next six months. Kwok surrendered at Penampang on December 19, in the hope of saving his people and stop the hunt for the rest of the resistance. But his hope was in vain – the Japanese sentenced many to death. Altogether, the brief uprising cost some 1,000 lives.

The Japanese Occupation finally came to an end in 1945. Jesselton was lucky to have three buildings standing after Allied troops bombed the Japanese into submission. These buildings – the Clock Tower, the old General Post Office and the Welfare building – still stand today. The Clock Tower dates back to 1905 while the other two were constructed in 1918 and the 1920s respectively.

The end of the war marked Jesselton's rise as Sabah's capital, replacing Sandakan in the east. Jesselton, renamed Kota Kinabalu in 1967, remains the headquarters of the West Coast Division.

As a state of the Federation of Malaysia, Sabah is administered under the Federal and State Constitutions. A Legislative Assembly looks after matters over which the Federal Constitution has no jurisdiction. The State Constitution provides for a Head of State *(Yang di-Pertua Negeri)* whom the Malaysian Supreme Ruler *(His Majesty, The Yang di-Pertuan Agong)* appoints after consultations with Sabah's Chief Minister.

A Cabinet of comprising a Chief Minister and eight ministers run the State Government. Assisting them in their respective portfolios are assistant ministers. The day-to-day running of the state is carried out by both States and Federal officials. At district level, certain official duties are delegated to District Officers as well as District and Native Chiefs. Most of the civil servants in the state are now Sabahans sharing a common aim of improving the people's standard of living. Amenities like roads, schools, clinics, electricity and water supply continue to reach the people.

Sabah's narrow coasts comprise alluvial plains of good agricultural potential with the West Coast plains being the most developed. Here, paddy is the main crop.

Thirty-two per cent of Sabah's population live in the West Coast Division. They are mainly Kadazans, Bajaus and Chinese, spread over the districts of Kota Belud, Ranau, Papar, Tuaran and Penampang. They consist of farmers, businessmen, civil servants, traders, shopkeepers and others.

The Kadazans farm much of the fields in the West Coast Plains. Many of them are Christians today due to missionary efforts. With the arrival of the British and the coming of Christianity, many of the old habits such as head hunting among the Kadazans and Muruts ceased. But old customs still exist today in ritual forms.

Priestesses called *bobolians* or *bobohizans* (depending on dialect) play a major role in Kadazan ceremonial rituals. They are healers engaged to exorcize sickness brought by evil spirits. As mediums, they beseech harmful spirits to stay away from new born babies. At funerals, they head the rites that guide the deceased spirit towards its final journey up Mount Kinabalu. Incantations, prayers, singing, trances and animal sacrifice are common at these ceremonial rituals, some of which can last for days.

The Kadazan ceremony that has survived the introduction of religion, education and modernization is the annual harvest festival called *Magavau*, commonly known as *Pesta Menuai* in Sabah. It is held to give thanks to the *Bambazon* (spirits of the paddy) for a good harvest.

The ceremony begins with a priestess performing some rituals in a field where the rice has ripened. She collects seven well-ripened ears of rice and ties them together with a strip of black cloth. These ears of rice, known as *"bambazon do paai"* or rice souls, represent the necessity and continuation of life. The priestess then chooses seven ears of chaff and binds them with another strip of cloth – these signify the abstract needs of ancestral spirits. Then harvesting begins. Only when all the other rice stalks have been harvested in that field can the first seven ears be cut and taken home to the barn. The seven ears of chaff are left in the field. When the harvest is over, it is time for celebrations and the *Magavau* rites of thanksgiving and appeasement.

An atmosphere of goodwill pervails through-out the celebrations as the people extend their hospitality to everyone regardless of race or religion. Besides games, there are also beauty contests in which girls dressed in traditional black and gold Kadazan costumes participates. Feasting goes on and on and much *tapai* (fermented rice wine) is consumed.

Another important ceremony is the *Moginakan*, performed after a longhouse is built. Since not many traditional longhouses are built these days, the *Moginakan* is rarely performed. One of these last big ceremonies was held in Penampang in 1953. Many buffaloes, pigs and chickens were slaughtered for celebrations that lasted a whole week.

All over Sabah, particularly in the West Coast Division, colourful *tamus* are held once a week, usually on Sundays. *Tamus* are open air markets traditionally held by Kadazans, Muruts and Bajaus. Goods were once bartered but today, transactions are strictly cash. Nevertheless, the village folk still gather together with their wares as in the past – the Kadazans with their rice, fruits and vegetables, the Muruts, with their jungle produce such as rattan, resins and wild game; and the Bajaus with their fish, salt and cloth.

The biggest and perhaps best known *tamu* in Sabah is found in Kota Belud. Held on Sundays, it sells everything from buffaloes to betel nut and scores of products the city dwellers will find hard to identify. Almost always a medi-cine man is present to "entertain" the morning crowd with lengthy but interesting explanations about his potions.

Kota Belud is also the centre of the Bajau weaving industry producing colourful patterned jackets and fabrics sometimes used as a headdress by both the Kadazans and Bajaus. The Bajaus also make colourful food covers called *tudung saji*. The women sometimes balance these inverted *tudung saji* on their heads to carry things. These and other traditional crafts are being kept alive at the Kota Belud Handicraft Centre.

Bajaus were once seafarers but those in Kota Belud have since made Tempasuk Plain their home. Instead of fishing or bartering with other sea-borne traders for cloth and ironware, they now rear buffaloes and cattle and till the plains below Mount Kinabalu. Instead of riding the waves, they now ride horses – and skilfully too. However, some Bajaus living on the offshore islands are fishermen.

Like the land Bajaus, the Chinese on the West Coast have also adapted themselves extremely well. They have made a niche for themselves since the days of the Chartered Company rule. They have their own clan associations, schools and temples. This is not just in the West Coast but also in other parts of Sabah.

Four of Sabah's six public parks are situated in the West Coast Division. The most popular among them is the Kinabalu Park, the oldest park in Sabah and famed for the 4,101-metre granite mountain it takes its name from. Declared as a park in 1964, it is home to an amazing range of superlatives – the highest mountain in South-East Asia, the largest pitcher plant in the world, the largest flower, the most species of orchids and some of the rarest birds and animals. The 75,370-hectare park is also a botanical paradise – hundreds of plants from among its thousands are still waiting to be identified and classified.

Surprisingly, the mountain itself is one of Sabah's youngest areas. The massive granite rock only surged through the earth's crust only a million years ago, in time to have its crown sculptured by the last ice age 10,000 to 100,000 years ago.

Visitor accomodation, restaurants, an exhibit centre and the park headquarters sit in a mountain garden on the park's southern boundary. Situated about 1,520 metres above sea level, the garden holds an astounding variety of plants gathered from all levels of the park. The cool, highland location of the park also makes it a welcome break from the lowland heat. It is less than a two hour drive over a good road from Kota Kinabalu to the Park Headquarters. The park itself is the only place in the world where you can walk 4 to 5 miles and pass through tropical lowland forest to mountain alpine landscape and everything in between.

Even nearer to Kota Kinabalu – about half-an-hour by speed boat – is the Tunku Abdul Rahman Park, a sanctuary for the many beautiful species of coral and tropical fish found in the surrounding waters. Established in 1974, the 4,929-hectare park consists of five islands whose coral waters and powder-fine beaches are among its main attractions. On a good day, the calm seas are so clear that it is hard to tell where the air ends and the water begins.

Gaya is the largest of the five islands and the larger part of it belongs to the park. Where once stood a British trading station, an immigrant colony of Filipinos has spread over the sea. Beyond this corner is a parkland and Police Beach – a cove of sweeping white sand backed by jungle that can be explored through trails cut by the park authorities.

Pulau Tiga Park was established in 1978 and covers 15,864 hectares. Pulau Tiga has three large mud volcanoes, one of which is still active. Wild fruit trees and a stand of casuarina trees growing on a dormant volcano characterize the island. The fruit trees attract a variety of birds such as island pigeons. Other birds found here are the Frigates and the Megapodes which lay eggs in huge mounds of sand and rotting vegetation on the beach, leaving them to incubate on their own. The young are left to dig their way out and to fend for themselves.

The latest addition to the parks is the Crocker Range National Park. It takes up a fair chunk of the range that forms the backbone of Sabah, spilling over the borders of the West Coast Division into the Interior. It was declared a park in 1984 to protect the water catchment areas that feed the West Coast and Interior plains. The main road from Kota Kinabalu to Keningau runs through it, climbing as high as 1,700 metres with spectacular views along much of the way. Along the road at about 1,400 metres is an interesting private motel with a reputation for exotic dishes like wild boar and deer. The owner has landscaped the steep slopes around the motel into a mini-park with ponds.

4 *(previous page)* Kota Kinabalu, the state capital, lies on Gaya Bay and was originally known as Singgah Mata, a romantic Malay name meaning "where the eyes linger". Some of the locals, however, preferred to call it *Api-Api*, which means Fire! Fire!. But the British North Borneo Chartered Company, which set up a trading post along the bay, renamed it Jesselton in 1899 after Sir Charles Jessel, the company's vice-chairman. The city assumed its present name in late 1967. KK, as the city is popularly known, was demolished a few times, only to rise again like a phoenix. It is a relatively new city rebuilt after World War Two to replace Sandakan as the state capital.

5. The faithful are called to prayer from loudspeakers mounted on mosques' minarets. On the outskirts of Kota Kinabalu, the State Mosque retains an age-old serenity despite its contemporary Islamic construction. Inside, Muslims ritually cleanse their bodies by a landscaped pool before going for prayers. There they lend their voices to the sounds of prayer heard in many parts of the city.

6. Muslim children are taught Islam at an early age, particularly boys, who follow their fathers to the mosque for Friday prayers. Although Islam is the official religion, there is a surprising level of religious and racial tolerance among the many ethnic groups.

5   6
7

7 *(previous page)* Sabah has a small Indian Hindu community who worship at the Lok Kwai Temple, adjoining the Lok Kwai Army Garrison.

8 Kota Kinabalu's landmark is undoubtedly the 31-storey Sabah Foundation Building that stands beside the sea on Likas Bay. A cylindrical 72-sided polygon, this building with a glass facade has a revolving restaurant and houses the State Government's administrative offices. The Foundation was set up in 1966 to complement the State Government's efforts to improve the lives of the people. It has been responsible for, among other things, schools, scholarships, sports facilities, student hostels, flying medical services to the rural people, branch campuses of the Mara Institute of Technology and Universiti Kebangsaan Malaysia.

9 A hundred and five hectares of what was once a swamp in the Likas Bay area are now part of the Likas Sports Complex, equipped with a grand stadium, a gymnasium, tennis, badminton and squash courts, swimming pools and a clubhouse.

10 *(following page)* A close-up aerial view of Kota Kinabalu occupying a strip of land along Gaya Bay.

11 The Kota Kinabalu fish market is a wet maze of tables piled with gleaming fish, and ringing with voices shouting bargains.

12 Crayfish, scallops and crabs are some of the bounty from the seas around Sabah.

13 Both traditional and modern methods of fishing are used by Sabah fisherfolk. Small craft like this outboard-driven boat as well as large trawlers with cranes comb the seas daily.

14 Another section of the Kota Kinabalu market selling a variety of fresh vegetables. Displayed above the vegetables are dried foodstuff and local delicacies.

15. The Filipino community in Kota Kinabalu has manifested itself in a "market" of its own, just a stone's throw from the other two. Filipino handicrafts are sold here and tailoring services are offered on the sidewalks.

16 *(following page)* A bird's eye view of the capital picks out two of the city's most prominent land marks – the red and white roof of the Sabah Museum and the grey and gold facade of the State Mosque and the Majlis Ugama Islam Sabah (MUIS) Building. The Sabah Museum was completed in 1984. The design of its five-storey main building is adapted from the traditional longhouse.

14   15

17 Seven kilometres south of Kota Kinabalu lies Tanjung Aru, the capital's beach and parkland playground. Situated on land reclaimed from the sea is a plush beach resort hotel. Boats here ferry visitors to and from Tunku Abdul Rahman Park, just offshore. At low tide, the long beach here becomes a popular hunting ground, combed by locals for edible bivalves.

18 Daybreak lifts a veil of clouds to reveal Mount Kinabalu's shadowy silhouette around which Kota Kinabalu's changing skyline pivots. The majestic mountain can be seen from most parts of Sabah but yet seems to guard her mysterious charms from the twentieth century. In the foreground is the Tanjung Aru Mariner.

19 *(following page)* A close-up view of a feather star, a common invertebrate fauna in the waters off Sabah.

17   18

20 A diver's haven, the Tunku Abdul Rahman Park was set around five islands (Pulau Manukan, Pulau Mamutik, Pulau Sulug, Pulau Sapi and Pulau Gaya) in 1974 to protect the marine life in the waters from being depleted by fishermen using home-made bombs. While Australia's Great Barrier Reef may be the most famous, Malaysian reefs probably have as many coral varieties. The Park operates glass-bottomed boat rides over the coral wonderland for the curious.

Photographed here is Pulau Manukan, stretching lanquidly in the sun. Weekenders come to picnic on her shores and frolic with masks and snorkel in the crystal clear waters, those who do not fancy the water can bird-watch or stroll in the jungle trails.

21 Many of the minute spectacles in the sea go unobserved in the night, such as this tiny coral polyp. Its millions of ancestors form the core of coral reefs like the one it lives on.

22 Basking briefly in flashlight, a starfish smaller than the face of a diver's watch shows off its brilliant colours.

20   21

22

23 Besides shell-collectors, regular groups of scuba divers also frequent the waters of the park. Diving lessons are conducted here.

24 A fantasy of lacy fireworks exists 15 metres below, but you will have to look for it. Measuring just five centimetres across, this soft coral beauty could be missed.

25 A nocturnal animal, the orange tubestra is another minute coral specimen just three centimetres wide.

23 24
25

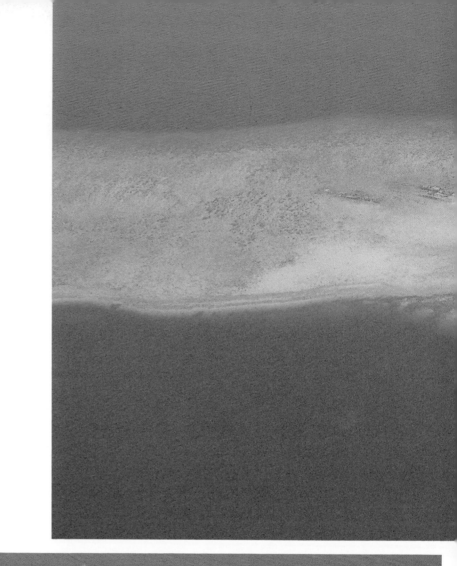

26 Solitude ... Pulau Sulug has plenty of it. Being furthest from shore, it has not been developed like the other islands in the Tunku Abdul Rahman Park. Its pristine condition is an attraction in itself.

27 If you have ever dreamed of living in an island home, Pulau Mamutik is where it can come true. A self-catering eight-person lodge is available from the Sabah Parks authorities for a modest rental. Here, one can see birds like the pied hornbill, found only on such offshore islands. Between September and April, flycatchers and warblers drop by on the island for a brief rest on their annual migration.

28 Hiding among anemone tentacles that would stun any other fish, the clown fish perform their symbiotic role with their animal host. The fish bring back bits of food for their host in return for protection. The fish eat a little of the anemone, enough to absorb the chemicals that identify the tentacles to one another and tell them not to sting them. In other words, the fish become "tentacles" to the anemone.

27

26　　28

29 31
30

29 A clown fish plays peek-a-boo among the tentacles of a sea anemone.

30 An underwater flashgun lights up the underside of a coral plate and picks out a brightly coloured parrot fish, a coral grazer, slumbering beneath.

31 Pulau Sapi is one of the park's most popular islands. It holds the park's headquarters and is well equipped with shelters, trails and toilets for visitors. An aerial view maps the island's coral locations.

32 The corner of Pulau Gaya closest to the mainland lies beyond the park boundaries. It's home to a growing community of Filipinos spreading their "floating" village across the water. The Sabah Government has taken steps to curb the growth of their settlement and to integrate them into society by providing them with housing, water supply and schools.

33 Police Bay lies on the northern shore of Pulau Gaya. About half an hour by speed boat from Kota Kinabalu, Police Bay and Police Beach are popular destinations for divers and picnickers or those who just want to snorkel close to the shore. It is also a starting point for a trek across Gaya.

34 Largest of the five islands in the Tunku Abdul Rahman Park, Pulau Gaya is covered by coastal forest threaded by a network of trails laid by the park authorities. An elevated plank walkway provides visitors with a closer look at the mangrove trees that thrive happily in mud and salt water. Cycads, primitive living fossils that look part fern, part palm, grow on rocky cliff areas and at the edge of sandy beaches. A lucky visitor might glimpse a pangolin, wild pig, macaque monkeys or monitor lizards.

32   34
33

35　37
36

35, 36 Mud volcanoes tend to spend a few active years "growing" forest. Activity might just resume years later at the same spot or nearby.

37 "Tiga" means three in Bahasa Malaysia, Sabah's official language. And three is the number of mud volcanoes that make up Pulau Tiga, the main island of Pulau Tiga Park. The light blot on the island's jungle green canopy marks the spot of a violent eruption in 1949 which caused underground gas from one volcano to ignite and burn for weeks. Today, only one of the volcanoes is still active and continues to bubble gas and mud. Very often, the mud bubbles out of the ground quite harmlessly. The island was gazetted as a park in 1978 not just for its geological importance but also for its animal life such as the spectacular frigate birds and peculiar megapode.

38 Papar is a sleepy coastal town 20 kilometres west of Kota Kinabalu. It is from here in 1881 that Roman Catholic missionaries started spreading both religion and education to Sabah. Before the West Coast Highway was built in the 1960s, the railway was the only link between it and Jesselton. It ran over the Papar River where it came close to oblivion when Allied forces planted bombs at the base of its bridges during the Japanese Occupation in 1941 – 1945.

39 A tombstone behind the Kimanis Estate is all that is left as a reminder of Sabah's first American colony at Kimanis. Thomas B. Harris, the chief secretary of the American Venture died of malaria in 1866 and this simple tombstone is said to have been cut in Hong Kong, shipped over and hauled across the colony by buffalo.

38   39

40   41

40 In total solitude ... a Kadazan lady prays in the cool and serene St. Michael's Church in Penampang. This stone church was completed in 1949, ready for use on Easter Sunday.

41 Exterior view of the St. Michael's Church.

42 *(following page)* Reflecting a pleasure in preserving their cultural heritage, Kadazan girls don their traditional costume during a local festival. Split bamboo and rattan are painstakingly woven to form the sunshade hats with designs that subtly signal ethnic identities.

43

43 Rice forms the staple of the Kadazan diet. While the Muruts and other indigenous people also grow rice, the Kadazans were the first to use the plough. With it, they have tilled the plains of the coast and the interior. Kadazan resourcefulness was first noted by the British in 1885. The plough is still used today, where with a little modification to the plough, babysitting and ploughing can be done simultaneously and with ease too.

44

44 In Kadazan paddy fields around Kinarut and Penampang, a wooden monument stands alone. These monuments, called *sininggazanaks* were a common sight at the turn of the century. They were used to commemorate the death of a childless person, planted on the property of the deceased by a family member most likely to inherit the land. Standing about two metres tall, this *sininggazanak* is carved in distinctive Kadazan style out of a single log of hardwood.

45 Tamparuli lies 47 kilometres north of where the coast road branches for Ranau and Kota Belud. Serenity highlights most days in this Kadazan community of mellow paddy fields and wandering buffaloes. This small town's claim to fame lies in a popular local Kadazan song which sings of its long swing bridge. The song has been translated into many languages.

46 In Tamparuli, one can see a fine example of the typical suspension bridges across many of Sabah's rivers. Crossing one is not for the nervous. Nowadays, metal cables and wire netting have since replaced or reinforced the traditional structure of wood, rattan and rope, but they do not stop the bridge from swinging under the footfall of pedestrians.

45   46

47 Tuaran is an agricultural district which boasts of the largest research station in Sabah – the Tuaran Agricultural Research Centre. Studies on pest and disease control and different strains of paddy and other food crops are undertaken here. A large lotus pond can be found in the district at Telipok, where water hyacinth is also grown for feeding pigs.

48 A Kadazan wedding sees a rare airing of traditional instruments such as the bronze *kulintangan* (gongs) and *gendang* (drums) made of wood and calf skin. These women are playing an instrumental piece called the *Tundarikoton*.

49 *(following page)* Kota Belud is the name synonymous with its *tamu* – Sabah's traditional open-air market. Aside from the weekend buzz the *tamu* creates, Kota Belud is a small rural riverine town nestling at the foot of Mount Kinablu where life seems to grind to a halt before sunset. It's Bajau country where herds of cattle and buffalo range the nearby Tempasuk Plains.

50 *(following page)* All manner of things lie neatly piled on the ground – wild honey, vegetables, game meats, fish, tobacco. People laugh, haggle and chat. It is Sunday and this is the orderly chaos of the Kota Belud *tamu* – the biggest around. More than just a weekly market, this traditional affair is also a cultural and social event of Sabah's rural people, as yet spared by the State's march to progress.

51 *(following page)* Buffaloes mean money. Valued at about M$1,000 each, they are a measure of a family's wealth and many dowries asked include a few buffaloes in their price. At the Kota Belud *tamu*, a Bajau rides his heard into a noisy auction for slaughter, breeding or export. Buffalo sales are a strictly male activity, like the corner reserved for cockfights.

52 *(following page) Tamu* days mean an opportunity to exchange gossip and observe the goings-on between different cultures when they come peacefully to buy and sell. The tobacco and betel nut chews enjoyed by these women are dying out in the face of a younger, educated generation who have begun to turn to twentieth century ideals of beatuy that do not include stained teeth.

53 With the passage of time, the ceremonial rituals of the Bajau people get increasingly rare. Skilled display of Bajau horsemanship has been reduced to appearances for occasions like state festivities. Aside from ceremony, these "Borneo cowboys" use horses for transporting and herding cattle. They were fine fishermen a few generations ago before they turned to life on land around Kota Belud. The Bajaus are Muslims believed to have emigrated from the Philippines, although they also claim descent from the Johor Malays. Legend tells of a Malay princess from Johor who was waylaid by the Sultan of Brunei as she was sailing to a Sulu prince. Her escort of war boats, fearing the Sultan of Johor's wrath, never returned home. Instead the guards wandered the seas and eventually became known as the Bajaus. They played a major role in the early days of the Brunei Sultanate with sea-power policies. They are believed to have married into Malay aristocracy.

54 A Bajau Horseman in ceremonial costume.

53　54

55 A colourful traditional Dusun wedding in Kota Belud. The wedding ceremony is usually accompanied by feasting and drinking *tapai* (rice or tropical wine).

56 The traditions of the Bajaus are fast disappearing. Photographed here is a rare scene of the Bajaus performing the *Runsai* dance.

57 Traditional Bajau costumes making an appearance during the singing of traditional music called *Isun-Isun*.

58 *(following page)* The Kota Belud paddy plain dubbed the "rice bowl of Sabah" unfurls at the foot of Mount Kinabalu. In spite of almost 100,000 acres given to paddy-farming, Sabah still imports rice. The National Paddy Board, a Federal agency, encourages farmers towards better yields by urging them to use fertilisers, growing improved paddy strains and double cropping, besides giving subsidies.

55 56
57

59 *(previous page)* A remote village in the interior of the Crocker Range.

60 Encompassing a unique, irreplaceable slice of nature over an area as large as the island of Singapore, Kinabalu Park was established in 1964 across lowland rainforests, montane forests, cloud forest and sub-alpine meadow before culminating in Mount Kinabalu's granite peak at 4,101 metres. More than just a pretty recreational spot in the cool heights of the Crocker Range, the park's centre is also a place to learn. Slide-shows, guided walks and exhibits reach out to visitors and the park's mobile unit brings documentaries to local villages. A herbarium and mountain garden have been created for botanical studies. Besides preserving a natural heritage for the future, the park also protects western Sabah's watershed. Mount Kinabalu feeds eight major rivers that bring water for drinking, fishing and irrigation to many Sabah towns and villages.

61 Smaller wildlife in the park are easier to spot than the larger, shy animals. This female Trilobite beetle keeps its larval shape for life and feeds on decaying wood.

60　61

　　62

63   64   65

62 *(previous page)* Amazingly, not much is known about the orchids of the Kinabalu Park although some 1,500 species garland the forests with their cascades of flowers. A reference collection has been established at the park to remedy that gap. Enthusiastic orchid growers and commercial orchid enterprises in Kota Kinabalu, Tawau and Labuan have helped create an awareness about these plants and boost their breeding and hybridization.

63 Kinabalu's Park's humid lowland is home to the world's largest flower – *Rafflesia*. This speckled beauty usually measures half-metre across, although the largest of this genus can grow up to a metre in diameter. A dozen species are known to exist, all in South East Asia. Growing without leaves or roots, this parasitic flower sucks life from trailing forest wines. It blooms with a strong odour of rotting meat, attracting

flies which pollinate it. The flower then shrivels up and waits for the rain to wash its many tiny seeds out to other vines.

64 Four hundred and fifty species of fern have been listed in Kinabalu Park against 10,000 known in the world. As many fern species exist here as in the whole of Africa, adapted to growth on the ground, in shade, open sun or high up in trees.

65 Once profuse along mountain trails between 1,500 – 3,500 metres, the pitcher plant has fallen prey to visitors who collect them out of curiosity although this is against park's regulations. Pitcher plants thrive on poor soil, getting whatever nourishment they need by trapping insects in their stomach-like pitchers filled with digestive juices. The pitcher is really a marvellously modified leaf. The largest ones are known to have drowned rats.

66 *(previous page)* An aerial view of Kinabalu South showing the 'tourist trail' from Laban Rata Resthouse to the summit. Sayat-Sayat huts can just be seen below the clouds. The grooved and polished Panar Laban rock face on the left of Sayat-Sayat huts is a result of glaciation during the last Ice Age.

67 Trekkers gladly take a breather from their laboured going at Sayat-Sayat, one of the more popular huts to stay. It is closest to the summit which means climbers do not have to resume trekking in the middle of the night to get to the top by dawn.

68 Ropes guide climbers safely up and down the pitted rock slope of the summit.

69 If you are fortunate, you can reach South Peak on a clear blue day. The weather is fickle with the mountain, one moment brilliant sunshine, next misty and cloud signalling a drenching. This alternate heating and cooling is responsible for causing thin layer of rock to flake off the granite face, giving the summit a tiled look.

70 An aerial view of Kinabalu East showing the jagged peaks.

71 *(following page)* Peaks and pinnacles carved by ice during the last Ice Age rise out of the grey expanse of West Kinabalu's sloping semi-dome shaped Summit Plateau. Low's Peak at 4,101 metres is located at the top left of the picture.

72, 73 The ice that scoured Mount Kinabalu's granite face melted just 10,000 years ago. Since then, rain and wind have smoothed out features like this lion's head at Low's Gully. The gully is a glacier-cut, one-and-a-half kilometre deep U-shaped cleft. It cleaves the mountain into east and west halves. British explorer, Sir Hugh Low, was the first person who breached the summit area on March 11, 1857, with his Kadazan guide to gaze down the chasm that now bears his name. His was the first recorded ascent and records of his finds opened up a mountain treasure trove for scientists and adventurers alike.

74 *Leptospermum Recurvum*, a mountain gelam which occurs at higher attitudes.

75 *cf Vaccinium sp*, a scrub species growing on the slopes of Mount Kinabalu.

72   73
    74 75

76 *(previous page)* Low's Peak at 4,101 metres is the highest peak on the summit of Mount Kinabalu. Early morning sun-rays bathe Low's Peak accentuating the jagged peak which is due to their being fractured by the alternate freezing and thawing of water in cracks in more recent times during the Pleistocene Period.

77 A bird's eye view of the nine million-year old mist-shrouded Mount Kinabalu massif that is still rising at a rate of five millimetres a year. This majestic mountain has been regarded as one of the most wonderful mountains of the world. Rising out of a tropical rain-forest to the summit, it has its own climate — a constant flux of clouds and wind, rain and cold and the warmth from the forests below.

78 A rare close-up aerial view of the Carson Falls in Kinabalu Park. This Fall is 1,606 metres above sea-level and tumbles down 120 metres below. From Timpohan Gate, the summit trail passes by the Carson's Fall, a waterfall named after the first warden of Kinabalu Park. This Fall is visible from the road leading to the Park Headquarters.

77   78

79 Native lady with load of farm produce on the head.

80 Kundasang lies 150km from Kota Kinabalu. A poetry of mountain and valley vistas spill from the edge of the Crocker Range that the road winds on. It is no wonder holiday-makers and tourists wend their way up'when they can. Two hours of pleasant drive brings you to Kundasang where the air is clear and fresh vegetables waiting to be brought.

79   80

81 Perkasa Hotel commands a good view of Mount Kinabalu and Kundasang. The 72-room hotel and convention centre is an alternative to the Kinabalu Park's chalets and hostel-type accommodation.

82 Water sprays come twirling on in the late afternoon, quenching the fields. Settled farming has replaced shifting cultivation at Kundasang and modern methods are fast moving in with the use of fertilisers and pesticides for better crops.

83 Farming folk at Kundasang haul their produce up to the main highway for sale at simple zinc and wood stalls. Freshly picked tomatoes, potatoes, corn, lettuce, brinjals and asparagus line the shelves.

81   83
82

84 There are no Kadazan milkmaids in Kundasang. Milking has been mechanized and milk goes straight into processing and eventually ends up flavoured, bagged and distributed. A special supply goes to local schools.

85 The cool temperate climate in the Kundasang areas with its lush grassland lends itself not only to market gardening but also to dairy farming. The Tenusu Dairy Project is but one of the dairy projects in the area.

86 A small horse calls to another across a dairy field in Kundasang. Its lonely cry seems to hark back to Sabah's disappearing frontiers as farms and dairies replace the forests.

84   86
85

87 *(previous page)* "It's Switzerland" says an observer gazing wide-eyed at Kundasang's pasture land. Here, the grass is rich, thick and sweet smelling and the air is bracing. And with the mountain looming in the background, it is possible to believe that you are not in the tropics but in some Alpine meadow, not in the tropics.

88 An unlikely scene unfolds at 1,500 metres on the Pinosuk Plateau in Kundasang. It's a golf course at the Mount Kinabalu Golf Course Complex. Golfers here can glean inspiration for their game from the sacred mountain itself. Also in the works are a club house, restaurant, swimming pool, squash and tennis courts – good distractions to have around when the course gets misted over by clouds perhaps.

89 A weathered boulder lies on the manicured grass at the golf course as a reminder that this is Kinabalu country.

90 Healing effects of a steaming sulphurous spring is another draw at Kinabalu Park. Developed by the Japanese during World War Two, the Poring Hot Springs is a 43-kilometre ride from the Kinabalu Park headquarters over tortuous road that makes a hot bath an especially recuperative luxury, if you do not already need one after scaling Mount Kinabalu. Tiled tubs have replaced the wooden Japanese ones and taps give a personal combination of hot spring and cold stream water. Photographed here is a swimming pool.

covery of oil in the Kudat Peninsula by Franz Witti, an explorer hired by the Chartered Company, in 1880 and 1881.

Kudat has a good natural harbour. There were hopes that it would prosper as a major port on the trade routes between China and Europe. William H. Treacher, the first Governor of Sabah, moved the country's administrative centre from Labuan to Kudat. But the British had not reckoned on piracy nor the shortage of drinking water at that time. Because of these factors, Kudat lost its capital status to Sandakan in 1883.

That year also saw the migration of 96 Christian Hakkas to Kudat. They spurned the opium smoking habit of the other Chinese immigrants and turned their energies towards planting paddy and vegetables. More Chinese followed encouraged by the free passages from China given by the Chartered Company along with land, vegetable seeds and loans of money. Vegetable farming boomed as the Chinese established themselves in the area and exported their produce to Sandakan.

More than a century has lapsed since the founding of Kudat. The uncontrolled growth of the timber industry and widespread shifting cultivation by the tribal people have resulted in bare hills and scrub country. The authorities have since embarked on an extensive reforestation programme to restock this dwindling timber supply and at the same time, help to contain soil erosion. To supplement this reforestation effort, various short-term and long term programmes are also carried out and these include encouraging the tribal people to switch to settled farming.

The way of life of the Rungus, a sub group of the Kadazan or Dusun has been affected. Although they have managed to retain more of their old ways than many other tribes, only a few of them now live in the last of the old-style longhouses. Aging longhouses are being demolished and replaced by new onces with zinc instead of *attap* roofs.

Although many of Sabah's Kadazan or Dusuns are either Christians or Muslims, many of the Rungus still hold animistic and spiritual beliefs. They believe that the universe has both good and bad spirits responsible for situations like birth, death, disease, drought, flood and successful crops. They also believe in the existence of an hierarchy of supernatural beings. At the top of the hierarchy are the celestial deities, followed by the household and earth deities. Each level is in charge of a specific task in human life or the universe.

Of the celestial deities, the *Kinoringan* is seen as creator of all. He and his wife *Sinumundu* are said to have made the human race and the universe. The Rungus call him through a "priest", a male ritual specialist, whenever they need him to intervene during community crises like epidemics, floods, drought or crop failures. *Kinoringan* also watches over wars and marriages. Other deities concerned with other aspects of human life are reached through a "priestess".

Bintingavan, *Sombila* and *Aki Molohing* are some household deities. The *Binting* is a spirit of the sky and it ranks above the *Sombila* which lives in the house. It is the head of all bad spirits and ensures that *Sombila* does not harm the people. *Aki Molohing*, which lives in the kitchen, is the protector and carrier of good fortune. The Rungus remember these spirits at major festivals.

Among the numerous earth deities are *Mogundahali* and *Ansamung* which live on earth as spirits of the jungle, trees, sea, water, paddy fields and rocks. Only when someone is ill or an unexpected problem occurs in a family is a priestess called to find and pacify the particular spirit.

Spirits of life-sustaining water, fields and jungle are remembered at a general sacrificial festival called *Moginum* which takes place once every three to seven years. It is an expensive festival involving at least eight pigs and ten chickens for slaughter and other ceremonial items like plants, flowers and fish. The five-day worship is led by a priestess.

The Rungus have no calendar. They note the passing of the years by rice seasons. Life revolves around paddy and the three stages of preparing the fields, planting and harvesting. Fields are usually prepared in July, the beginning of the Rungus year, while harvest usually comes in May culminating in the annual harvest festival the Rungus called *Mongulok*.

A different type of people who call themselves "Bonggi" but who are usually referred to as the Banggi Dusun inhabit the islands of Banggi and Balambangan. The word Dusun is a misnomer as their language is not even closely related to the Kadazan or Dusun language group, About twenty years ago the government persuaded some of them to live and work in coconut plantations in a bid to stop their shifting cultivation habit.

Coconut plantations are also found on the mainland along with rubber which the British brought to Malaysia. Since Sabah's independence, oil palm and cocoa have boosted the area's agricultural potential.

The beaches here are among some of the best in Sabah. The islands of Banggi, Balambangan and little Tigabu surface from the seas like a dream, laced with coral reefs. Like dreams, these areas are not easy to reach. Few people are sufficiently motivated by the pristine beauty to brave the distance and lack of amenities for the experience.

Perhaps this is a blessing in disguise to ensure that the countryside, untrammelled sands and the guileless ways of the Rungus remain unspoilt a little longer.

93 Kudat town is more than a hundred years old. Rebuilt after World War Two like most of Sabah's towns and cities, its modern appearance belies the gentle pace of life there as divisional headquarters of the Kudat, Pitas and Kota Marudu districts, and the islands of Balambangan and Banggi.

94 A Rungus man with tobacco and betel nut stained teeth, head swatched with colourful headgear and a warm smile.

95, 96 Big or small, *tamus* or open market sprout wherever people need to trade. The Kudat *tamu* is a meeting place of the Rungus from different villages and other local ethnic groups.

97 With a towel for a casual headgear and a twinkle in her eyes, an old Rungus lady continues to make her way to the *tamu* with her *wakid* (bamboo basket) and cheerfully sets up shop on the market ground.

94   96   97
95

98   100
99

98 Traditional Rungus life is a communal one shared by many families in a longhouse with their dogs and farm animals. A common gallery sees their laundry hung to dry, and activities like winnowing, mat-making, beadwork being done.

99 Longhouses always seem to overflow with children. The Rungus children pictured here look out at the world with an innocent confidence not shared by the youngest ones.

100 Zinc has replaced thatch in new longhouses erected by the State Government for the Rungus people.

101 There are only two villages and a few scattered houses on Balambangan Island. Fishermen use them for only part of the year, moving back to other villages either on Banggi Island or the mainland when fishing is not good or after drying their catch. Cultivation has laid bare part of the island and large limestone outcrops can be found on its southern end. Hardly anything remains of the old East India trading post at Tanjung Periok, midway along the east coast. Access to it is blocked by a strip of mangrove and pandan swamp which could only have been wilder and wider at the turn of the 19th century.

102 Only a few Chinese egrets *(Egretta eulophotes)* exist today as colonies of them were killed for their plumes at the end of the 19th century. Native to China, the bird was possibly a common winter visitor to Borneo once, when scores of them could be seen in coastal areas like this.

103 Bak Bak Beach, 10km from Kudat, is a favourite haunt of the local people for fishing, swimming and picnicking. Other beaches in the residency include the rather remote Sikuati and Bangau beaches.

101 102
103

Chapter Four

THE SANDAKAN DIVISION

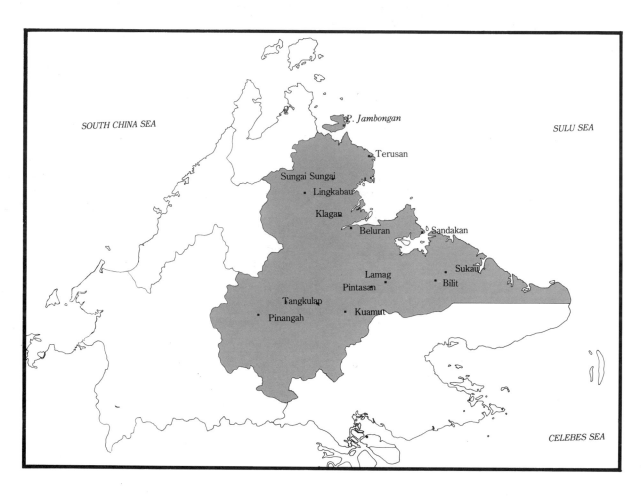

The success story of Sandakan as one of Sabah's earliest towns is without rival. William Clark Cowie, a Scotsman working for a German in Singapore, was running guns to Jolo through the Spanish blockade from Labuan. But Labuan harboured a Spanish agent and often Cowie and his adventurers were surprised by the Spanish and had their cargoes taken. Because of this Cowie obtained permission from his friend the Sultan of Sulu to use Sandakan Bay.

He set up his base at Pulau Timbang (Timbang Island) in Sandakan Bay. Cowie dubbed his gun running centre Sandakan, a 200-year-old Suluk name which mysteriously means "the place that was pawned". The name did not stick, however, as the locals preferred to call it Kampong German (German Village) because of Cowie's German colleagues' frequent visits. Twenty years later after his return to England he eventually became Managing Director and

then Chairman of the Chartered Company.

Meanwhile, Baron Von Overbeck's partners – the Dent Brothers – were trying to engineer a Royal Charter to administer the large tract of land ceded to them by the Sultans of Brunei and Sulu in order to administer and develop the territory. In February 1878, Overbeck put William Pryer in Sandakan along with four other staff and gave him a title, Resident of the East Coast. William Hood Treacher, an administrator and often acting Governor of Labuan appointed Pryer as Consular agent, the Union Jack was then hoisted at Sandakan as the British era began.

When they arrived, there were only three villages in Sandakan Bay – Oopak, a Bajau village, Timbang, which was run by Suluks, and Kampong German. The latter, with only 17 houses, was the business centre of the area with a mixed population that included Arabs and Chinese. The latter were pre-occupied with trading of edible birds' nests and seed pearls.

Pryer set to work with his staff – two Chinese boys, a West Indian and a half-caste Hindu. He had an unenviable task of organizing and developing the area, and managing people who had never known formal administration. But he was sensitive to the natives and won their support in a surprisingly short time. He sorted their disputes, confronted pirate raids and dealt with slavery cases.

The ultimate test to his leadership came when a Spanish warship sailed into Sandakan Bay in September 1878 and threatened to take over the town. Pryer gathered the native chiefs and together they protested by deploying as many armed men about as they could. Pryer then invited the two Spanish captains to tiffin in the village where he casually mentioned the hostile natives. The Spaniards left after a round of gin and bitters, intimating about returning with more men. But they never did.

During Pryer's absence Cowie had wanted to take over Sandakan in the name of the Sultan of Sulu. Pryer returned, the Suluks were hostile, but he managed to keep peace until Overbeck and Dent returned. Dent paid Cowie off, who returned to the Sultan of Sulu reporting all was well.

By this time, Pryer decided that the location of Kampong German was too vulnerable and thought of moving it. But before he could do anything, a fire accidentally started by a local man razed most of the town on June 15, 1879. This left Pryer with no choice but to move the town to a new location. Six days later, he felled the first tree at Buli Sim Sim at Sandakan Harbour and earned himself credit as founder of Sandakan.

The new town sat between the water's edge and the jungle and was called "Elopura", meaning beautiful city. In 1881, Pryer became the town's first Resident under Chartered Company Rule.

Part of the town was perched on the steep hill slopes that ended abruptly at sea. The rest of it was built on stilts over water. Split palm tree trunks were streets that bridged the attap-thatched sea-houses to land. European bungalows sat on terraced hills. Official government buildings hugged the heart of town and tumble-down wooden huts made up Chinese and Malay shops. The town flourished in spite of the fact that the only way in and out was by sea.

In 1883, the town became Sabah's second capital and was firmly known as Sandakan again. Being the capital injected more verve into Sandakan. It soon became Sabah's busiest port with steam launches, smaller fishing craft and native boats cramming its wharves. Some sailed upriver to estates carrying livestock, furniture, beer, food and building material. Despite the tremendous amount of trade, there were no wheeled vehicles in Sandakan then. Goods were carried about on bent backs and strung from poles suspended between the shoulders of two men.

Pryer believed that Sandakan's success lay in its land. He enthusiastically encouraged experiments in planting rubber, cocoa, sago, coffee, manila hemp, bananas and coconuts on Sandakan's estates.

However, in 1886, Sandakan was devastated by a fire – only to be rebuilt more vibrant than before. Better houses with tiled or corrugated iron roofs were built followed by a hotel, a Chinese temple, an Anglican Church, a Roman Catholic mission, a mosque and a Sikh temple.

Education arrived with the setting up of several schools. St. Mary's Primary School – Sabah's first school – was pioneered by Roman Catholics in 1883, followed four years later by St. Michael's Boys School. These schools eventually drew students from all over Sabah, including one boy from the west coast who grew up to forge Sabah's independence – the late Tun Fuad Stephens. Meanwhile, the town continued to attract a spectrum of people – Ibans, Malays, Singaporeans, Javanese, Chinese, Indians, Europeans.

An 1891 census of occupations reflected its razzle-dazzle life – Chinese actors, gamblers, brothel-keepers, Chinese and Japanese prostitutes and prisoners of all races. Away from the dubious limelight, there were cobblers, carpenters, dhobies (laundrymen), butchers, bakers and traders.

Sandakan's main trading partners were Hong Kong and Singapore. The expected Chinese influx that ensued made the Chinese a big part of the town's people. Sandakan was nicknamed "Little Hong Kong of Borneo" as the clatter of mahjong became familiar.

Festivals like Chinese New Year became an affair shared by the whole town. Muslims like the Suluks, Bajaus, Malays, Bruneis and Indonesians brought with them their Hari Raya Puasa and Hari Raya Haji celebrations. The English community, in their inimitable style, settled into a very "proper" life that revolved around tea and tennis at the Sandakan Club, set up in 1884.

At the turn of the century, Sandakan had begun to resemble a prosperous colony – the jungle was restrained, roads were metalled and ponies were shod.

Sabah's wealth was, and still is, its timber resources. The first export shipment of timber from Sandakan in 1885 was quite an "accident". An Australian, De Lissa, arrived in Sandakan hoping to grow sugar cane on 40,000 hectares of estates. But world demand for sugar hit the doldrums and De Lissa ended up shipping timber to Australia. His load of Serayah wood sparked off Sabah's timber industry.

But Australia was not to be the main market. Hong

Kong took that title. With the opening of China and the expansion of rail roads, sleepers were needed. The British North Borneo Trading and Planting Company opened up the first efficient sawmill and Sabah's hardwood, Billian, was cut and exported. By 1890 the company employed more people than the government. The value of timber exports climbed as Chinese timber *towkays* clamoured for licences. But timber only really came into its own as the core of Sabah's economy after World War Two.

Tobacco vied with timber as a major export shortly after it was grown amidst misgivings on sugar cane estates near Sandakan in the early 1880s. The first few bales sent to London and later sold in Amsterdam were declared among the world's best. Dutch and German planters rushed to Sandakan to find their fortune in tobacco. By 1890, 61 tobacco estates were established across the land.

However, hopes of turning tobacco into money went up in smoke when the United States of America, the chief buyer, imposed a stiff tariff on imported tobacco. Prices fell, estates closed and tobacco's trade prominence plummeted. It did rise again but the few estates that were left prospered and by 1902 exports reached their highest ever figure. After that the industry declined slowly. Today, tobacco is still grown but it is mainly for local consumption.

Rubber stepped in to replace tobacco as number two in the export ranks. The first seedlings took root at the government experimental garden in 1882 – but only to provide shade. The first commercial trials were undertaken in 1892 on 20 hectares of land in Bongaya on the Labuk River.

In 1905, the government decided to encourage rubber planting by guaranteeing that no tax or levy would be introduced for 50 years. Twelve companies jumped at the incentives and within two years, rubber trees sprouted over 120 hectares of land. A decade later, the area expanded more than tenfold.

The end of World War One in 1918 also saw the end of many rubber estates. Prices plunged and the industry languished. Like tobacco, few estates survived those years.

One of Sandakan's prized products is birds' nests. These edible nests, found in abundance in the Gomantong Caves, about 32 km across Sandakan Bay, were discovered by the Idahans and Orang Sungei over 200 years ago. Also found here are fragments of Chinese artefacts at ancient cave burial grounds.

An Orang Sungei folk tale tells how the Gomantong Caves were discovered by one of their people. Many generations ago, an Orang Sungei hunter named Raja Tua Batulong wandered further than usual into the jungle with his spear and dog. Subsequently, he lost his way and walked aimlessly for days. On the ninth day, his dog took off after an animal. Batulong caught up to find it fighting with a

pig. He slew the pig and carved it up for food. As he was cutting up the pig, he discovered birds' nests inside the pig's stomach. The hunter ate his fill and went to sleep.

As he slept, he dreamt of seven fairies who came to his help. They gave him directions to a cave with many birds' nests called "Simund Hitam – Gomantong Besar." They told him to mark the cave so that he could find it again. He was also instructed to go on walking where he thought his village lay.

Batulong awoke and followed the directions. He found the cave just as they said and marked it with his shirt. Then he went on to a river where he was found by two men in a boat. They took him back to their village which lay upstream from Batulong's. The headman of the village fed, clothed and looked after Batulong till he was stronger.

As his strength returned, Batulong spoke of his dream, the cave and birds' nests. When he was well, he led the headman and his people to it. And that was how the Gomantong Caves were claimed by the Orang Sungei.

Simund Hitam is one of the two main caves in Gomantong. The other, the larger of the two caves, is Simund Putih. The two names refer to the main kind of birds' nests found in each cave – Simund Hitam for black nests and Simund Putih for white nests.

These caves have since been passed on to the people's descendants but the growing population led to some inheritance and ownership disagreements. The government stepped in to settle a major tussle in the late 19th century. Today, collecting rights are issued to the people by contract to prevent further disputes. Cave owners now jealously patrol their territories against poachers. Rituals are still performed every nest-collecting season to appease the spirits for permission to collect the nests.

Most of the birds' nests are exported to Singapore and Hong Kong. White nests made from pure saliva, by swiftlets are the most valuable. Unprocessed nests can sell for as much as M$1,500 per kilogramme. Cleaning, drying and ageing the nests for consumer sale could even triple the price. However, black nests – formed by saliva tainted with feathers and bits of plant – are worth much less.

After World War Two, Sabah's capital was moved from Sandakan to Jesselton, now renamed Kota Kinabalu. But Sandakan never lost the energy that made it such a vital town and port. It has developed rapidly over the years and is now Sabah's prime fishing port.

A 20-minute drive from the town is Sepilok, the world's largest *orangutan* sanctuary. Sabah is one of the world's last habitat of the endangered primate whose territory is shrinking because of the logging of forests for the timber industry. Laws have since been introduced to forbid the killing and capture of these *orangutans*.

To cope with *orangutans* orphaned during jungle clearing or those which have become too dependent on man through captivity, the Sabah Forest Department formed a Game Branch and set up the Sepilok Sanctuary in 1964. The sanctuary began as an experiment to help the *orangutans* return to their natural home by letting them live freely in jungle surroundings. Here, the *orangutans* are encouraged to climb, make nests, roam and forage in 4,000 hectares of forest reserve. On the way to or returning from Sepilok one can call in at the crocodile farms where you can see crocodiles from a few centimetres long to more than 3 metres.

Besides the *orangutans*, turtles in the Turtle Islands Park are also protected. The park, comprising three low, sandy islands known as Pulau Selingan, Bakkungan Kecil and Gulisan, is about a three-hour boat ride from Sandakan. There has been a turtle hatchery on Pulau Selingan since 1966. Eleven years later, Sabah Parks authorities declared the island a state park and set up hatcheries on the other islands. Before the park was gazetted, young turtles burrowing their way through more than half-a-metre of nesting sand to find their way to sea were either slaughtered for food, or skinned for their leather and shell.

104 *(previous page)* Modern, bustling Sandakan, one of Sabah's biggest, boldest cities, began as a fishing village that became a gun-running centre before developing into a trading post and a safe harbour for all. Fishing is still an important source of income for many residents. Sandakan is today the state's premier fishing port.

105 The timber industry in Sabah is not just about felling trees. The economics of its growth is guided by the Sabah Forest Development Authority (SAFODA), established in 1976.

106 Log ponds are a common sight near Sandakan harbour. Here, logs are kept awaiting shipment to Europe and Japan.

105   106

107 A lone tree stands out in a jungle no longer virgin. Much of Sabah's original forests have gone abroad, shipped out for the dollars that buy the state a place in the twentieth century. Fortunately, conservation has been recognized not only as being vital to Sabah's health and future, but also for the world. Land is still being set aside for preservation. Five of Sabah's national parks have been gazetted since 1974 thus preserving more than three million hectares of jungle.

108 Balancing racing Sabah's march of progress against the need for conservation, Sepilok takes its stance as the world's largest orang utan sanctuary, fighting to keep the jungle home for the primates. Orang utans have become victims of extensive logging, forest clearing the people who keep them illegally as pets. Sepilok helps the primates break their dependence on man and re-educate them in their jungle ways.

109 *(following page)* **110** *(following page 126) Orang utans* do not have the best table manners but milk-soaked muzzles do show that they enjoy their food. After a quarantine period to check on their health, they are slowly re-introduced to the jungle around Sepilok. Domesticated animals need a period of re-adjustment before they can successfully return to the wild. At the Sepilok sanctuary, newcomers after quarantine are allowed to mix with other *orang utans*, feed and exercise under supervision. Once comfortable with the place, people and other primates, they are allowed to mingle and exercise on their own, free to do the things that come naturally to an *orang utan*. When they are confident and healthy enough to fend for themselves, they are released in forests far from people.

111 The common tree frogs *(Rh pardalis Brumas)* have large stickly toe pads that help them cling on to tree branches. These amphibians often breed in water-clogged pot-holes along logging trials.

112 The krait wears its beautiful camouflage of colours as do many other snakes. Its secretive ways make it even harder to spot.

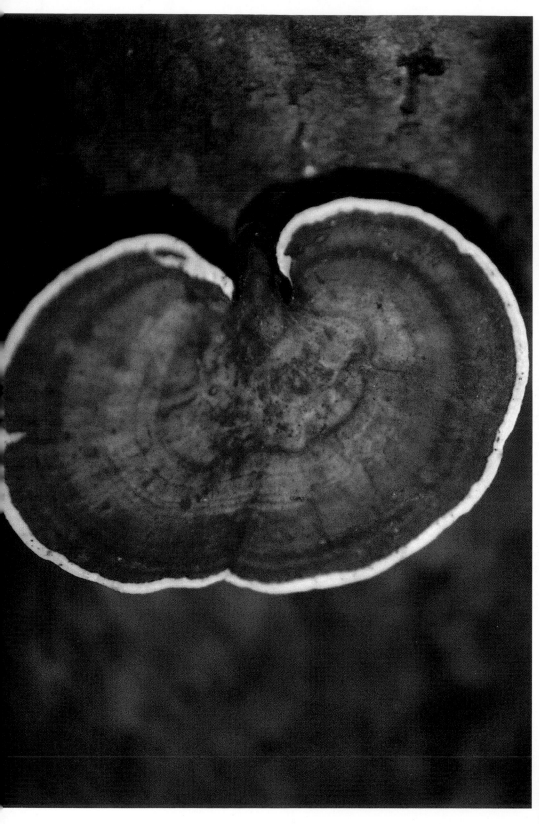

113 Humid lowland forests see a crop of fungi sprouting after a rainy spell. This one finds sustenance in a dead tree trunk.

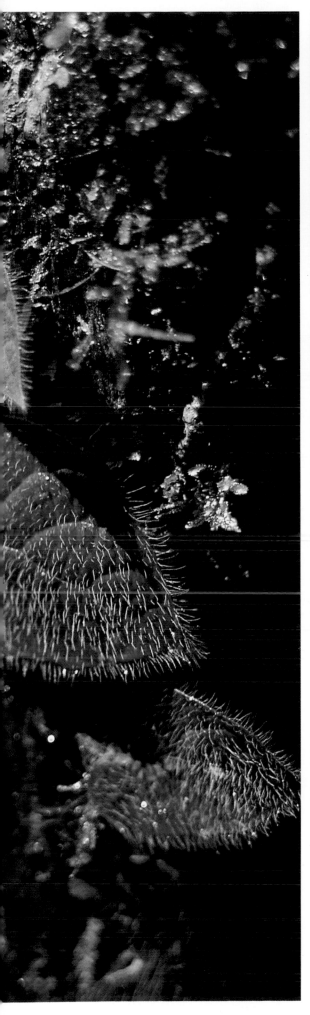

114 Moisture – epiphytes make the best of it. Their root are bared to air and not moist soil as they wend around trees, fighting for a foothold to reach life-giving light. Fortunately, water is something the rainforests are not often short of.

115 Fluffed up to resemble the fruit of the tree it sits on, the common Iora is familiar in gardens and open country throughout Sabah.

113   114   115

116   118
117

130

116 Life explodes in slow-motion as a mushroom blooms overnight. When fully grown, its cap can measure 18cm across.

117 This exotic bloom is borne by a common herb – ginger. The wild variety grows well in rainforests.

118 The common kingfishers *(Alcedo atthis)* are usually found along open water, and by ditches and ponds in open country but rarely seen on forest streams. A winter visitor to Borneo, they are usually seen perched bolt upright, or flying very swiftly and low over the surface of the water. They usually capture their food by plunging obliquely into the water from a suitable vantage point. Besides fish, they also feed on shrimps, ants, worms, paddy field crickets and insects.

119, 120 Huge oil palm plantations and small holdings have sown success for Sabah's agro-based economy. Oil palm ranks just behind cocoa in exports. Most of Sabah's raw palm oil is sent to Peninsular Malaysia while a small portion of the crude is refined at Sandakan for sale to Japan, Pakistan and India.

121 A close-up view of a big bunch of ripe oil palm fruit.

122 *(following page)* A daunting wall of rock shields a lovely strip of beach at Berhala Island from the pace of life at Sandakan beyond. The island has not always had an idyllic reputation. A leper colony was stationed on this island before World War Two and in 1942, the Japanese transported their prisoners there. The limestone cliffs here are more than 160 metres high.

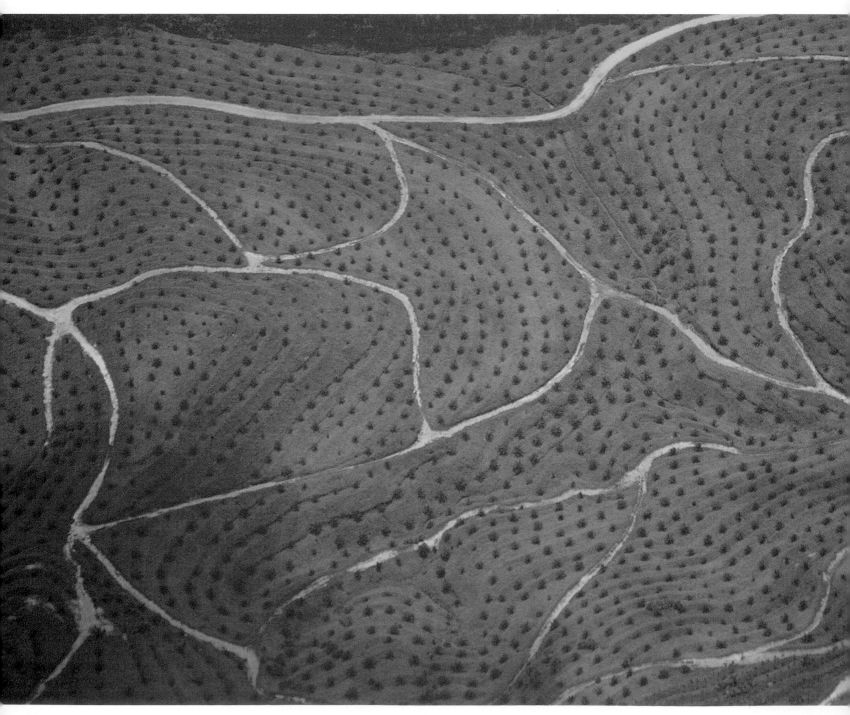

119 120 121

133

123   124

123 Pulau Selingan in the foreground is the largest of three islands north of Sandakan that make up the Turtle Islands Park, established by Sabah Parks in 1977. Here, the first turtle hatchery in Sabah was set up in 1966. Natives have long harvested turtle eggs on these islands for food and sale. But turtles are also hunted for food, their shells and skins, and their numbers have noticeably shrunk over the years Conservation has been stepped up, making hunting illegal and licences necessary for collecting eggs. Both green and hawksbill turtles lay their eggs in the park. Visitors can stay at Selingan's chalets to watch turtles laying eggs – the peak season being August to October – or newly-hatched turtles tunnelling their way out of the sand at the hatchery.

124 The green turtle *(Chelonia Mydas)* nests throughout the year on the islands of Pulau Selingan, Pulau Bakungan Kecil and Pulau Gulisan. Nesting is a laborious task for turtles. A hole almost a metre deep is dug and an average of about 100 eggs is laid before the nest is buried and the tracks covered. When this ritual is completed, the turtle returns to the sea.

The island's beaches are constantly under surveillance for nesting turtles. Nests are usually marked and eggs transplanted to hatcheries in the morning. At Selingan, eggs are carefully placed in sand pits about 73cm deep, buried and fenced up with wire mesh. Nests are tagged, noting date of collection, number of eggs and given a serial number of record. After 49 to 62 days, young turtles emerge and instinctively crowd at the side of the mesh closest to the sea. They are released soon after.

Chapter Five
THE TAWAU DIVISION

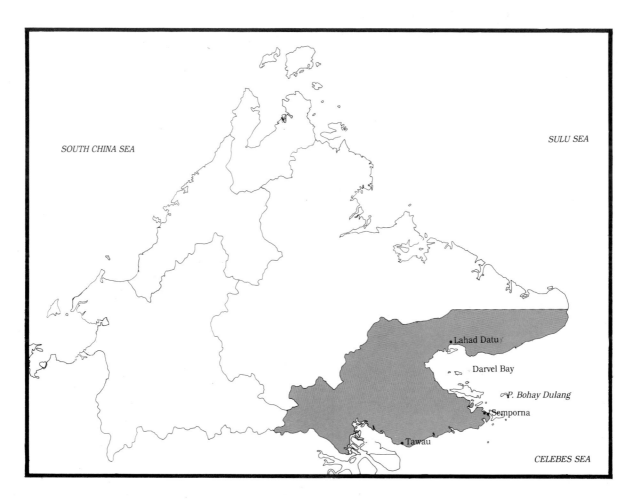

Sailing the seas off Sabah's east coast a century ago meant risking interception by pirates. And more often than not, the pirates would get away with cargo-laden ships. Crew and passengers were usually taken away as slaves – if they ever survived the attack.

But the British wanted trade to flourish in these waters. So after William Pryer had capably paved the way for peace and trade at Sandakan, he turned his attention south, towards Darvel Bay, the gateway to the rich hinterland that now lies beyond Tawau Division's main towns of Tawau, Lahad Datu and Semporna.

Pryer made his base at Silam, under the authority of Alfred Dent's company, shortly before it became the British North Borneo Company. It was easy getting the Idahans, Suluks and other local people to co-operate with him. But getting the sea-faring Bajaus to give their allegiance was not.

When the Chartered Company came to Sabah, it manifested itself in Darvel Bay in 1887 as a trading station which the Bajaus called *Tang Talon*, meaning "end of the jungle". William Crocker, then Acting Governor of Sabah, renamed it *Semporna*, a Malay word meaning 'perfect' a symbol of hope for the new town's future.

The name rang true for the Chinese who fled their homes in the Sulu islands under attack by the Spaniards. The Chinese were made welcome by the British who latter appointed their leader Toonah *"Kapitan China"*. As Captain of Semporna's first Chinese settlers, Toonah had the authority to solve his people's disputes and collect taxes on behalf of the Chartered Company. He wielded his position with power and influence among both Chinese and Suluks. With the better prices he offered, Semporna soon became the preferred place for trade at Darvel Bay.

The Bajau community swelled at Darvel Bay as traders

hawked their sea and jungle produce at Semporna and later settled at Silam and on the islands of Bum Bum, Larapan, Tatagan and Dinawan. Some even built permanent houses and planted paddy and coconuts.

Meanwhile, outright force by the British navy seemed the only way to keep renegade Bajaus in line. The Omadal Bajau persisted in preying on trading boats in the bay. The Bajaus at Semporna also grew restless after the Kapitan China died in 1895. Peace disintegrated between the Bajaus and Chinese. Shops were looted and the number of murders increased. The Chartered Company stepped in and settled the dispute with a dawn raid on the town by the navy in 1902. Murder suspects were rounded up and peace was subsequently restored.

It became clear to the British that the nomadic Bajaus has to be settled if authority over them were to be effective. Too often the Bajaus had given the law the slip by abandoning their makeshift homes and disappearing with their boats.

Licences were introduced for boats and to collect jungle produce. The movement of the Bajau could now be traced and owners of the boats identified. Buying the licences meant cash and slowly the Bajaus shed their subsistence way for a more settled one. They learned to build wooden houses on land instead of spending their lives adrift at sea. Boat-building skills brought new wealth to those who settled at Pulau Bum Bum. Others started planting paddy while those living in water villages maintained vegetable farms on land.

The Chartered Company created a new post of Native Chief to help it look after the affairs of the Bajaus. The first chief, a huge Bajau called Udang, succeeded in ensuring that the Company's scheme to relocate his people was carried out peacefully. Indeed, he went about his job with such loyalty that the British ceremoniously dubbed him "*Panglima*" or "*Warrior*" before his people. By 1909, peace had settled firmly and trade flowed smoothly in the Division.

The centre of the Tawau Division is Tawau, nicknamed the mini-boomtown. Founded in 1893, it has a good harbour and rich valley hinterland. Its main products are timber, cocoa, palm oil and rubber. In recent years, Tawau has wrested the title "Timber Town" from Sandakan. Aggressive reforestation has created Sabah's largest man-made timber forests at Tawau, Sabah Softwoods Plantation. Among the trees planted here is a fast growing species known as *Albizia falcataria*, which can grow to an amazing 30.5 metres in 64 months, a fact acknowledged by the Guinness Book of Records.

Even as Tawau's timber export outgrew Sandakan's, cocoa cultivation has become a lucrative business in this Division. In 1985, the crop ousted rubber as Sabah's second major crop, both in terms of cash and acreage. Tawau alone produced half the state's cocoa and this is possible because of one strong natural advantage – volcanic soil in the region. The Bukit Quoin Cocoa Research Centre has developed a high quality dry cocoa bean which is reported to be as good as beans from Ghana, Africa.

Cocoa was actually first planted in Sabah in the 1880s at the Agricultural Research Centre at Silam. It was however not thought that it could be a successful plantation crop. It surfaced again before World War Two but was abandoned. In 1955 only 80 acres were recorded as planted with cocoa. Its surge to the front of Sabah's economy has been phenomenal and timely. It is now Sabah's premier crop in terms of revenue.

Besides cocoa and timber, much oil palm is also grown in Tawau. Like cocoa, its rising exports have buffered losses in copra and hemp.

But it was tobacco that brought Lahad Datu to "life" in the late nineteenth century. The town, however, suffered when the price of the crop took a plunge during the 1930 global depression. After World War Two, prices for timber, oil palm and rubber revived.

Close to Lahad Datu are the Madai Caves. The Idahan people who have inherited the rights to collect the edible birds' nests live in villages near the caves. They are of the same ethnic group as the Orang Sungei and like their distant cousins, they too have stories to tell of how the caves came to be theirs.

One legend speaks of a man named Gomorid and his brother Siod, a dog. (People with animal siblings are not unusual in Borneo folktales. The idea forms the basis of some interesting folk-lores). Siod could speak like a man and hunt better than any dog. It could even bring down a rhinoceros or a bear. Its abilities reached the ear of the Sultan of Sulu, who decided he must have Siod. Ten men were then sent to get the dog. They were instructed to barter with Gomorid for Siod and if that failed, they were to take the dog by force.

Gomorid did not want to trade Siod, but the dog advised him to. The Sultan's men took Siod along with them but as they sailed past the Madai River, the dog slew seven of them. However, three were spared as a warning to the Sultan. Siod saw them off, then swam up the river, climbed Madai Hill and called Gomorid.

Gomorid heard Siod over the distance and set off with a spear and found his brother on top of the hill. Siod related to him what had happened. It also told him to remember Madai Hill and that Gomorid and his children would find riches in it. They left the hill and spied a golden deer at its foot. Siod and Gomorid gave chase.

They hunted for a long time but in vain. Eventually Siod stopped on top of Baturong Hill and waited for Gomorid to catch up. When he finally did, Siod told him to remember Baturong Hill and said that he and his children would find riches in it.

Again they spotted the deer. This time Gomorid wounded it with his spear but the deer ran on. After hunting the deer for a while, the brothers came to rest at Tapadong Hill. Again Siod told his brother to remember the hill. The deer reappeared and once more the brothers gave chase.

In this way, more hills were revealed to Gomorid, who finally gave up the hunt. Siod later slew the deer on top of Mount Kinabalu and discovered that it was made of solid gold. But the real value of the deer lay in the limestone hills it led the brothers over, hills that hold bird-nesting caves which would one day become a major source of native wealth.

True to the legend, the Idahan descendents are harvesting the caves today and the tales are still told in the evenings at the ramshackle village around Madai. The village is a seasonal campsite during harvest time.

Collecting season occurs twice a year for the black bird's nests – from April to May and October to November. About a month before the season sets in, the Idahans move to their camp to prepare their collecting equipment comprising flexible ladders made mostly from rattan, some wood and bamboo.

The bulk of the white bird's nests come from the caves around Tawau such as Baturong, Segarong and Tapadong. The nests are collected over three periods that fall in the first half of each year.

At Madai, Tapadong and Baturong too are sites of ancient civilization. The caves here were once used as burial grounds before Islam changed the habits of the people. The seasonal village of bird nesters at Madai have been built over archaeological remains as old as 10,000 years. The Idahans were initially suspicious of excavations suggested by the Sabah Museum, but relented in 1968 to cooperate willingly. Stone, bone and pottery artefacts were among the items unearthed in the area.

Over at Baturong is a limestone terrace called Hagop Bilo. It was a burial shelter where two simple log coffins were found along with three wooden statues about two metres tall. Carbon-14 dating indicates they are probably 1,000 years old. This terrace was also home to people many thousands of years ago.

While some Idahans still live solely off their bird's nests, most of them are now engaged in other trades. Many have moved away from their traditional hill paddy plots to grow cocoa, coconut and rubber. Others run taxis in towns and a few fall back on collecting jungle produce to supplement their income.

Clustered around the Semporna corner are islands standing on and along the edge of the continental shelf.

Geologically speaking, the area is still alive. Land and outcrops have risen and fallen in the recent geological times to create seas and islands where there were none before.

Semporna grew up on coral reef possibly 35,000 years old. Pulau Selangan is also made of raised reef limestone as ancient as Semporna's. The islands of Bohey Dulang and Bodgaya are the rocky northern rim of a flooded volcanic caldera. The sunken southern rim is marked by an arc of coral reefs in the shallow water.

The Kaya Pearl Company has taken advantages of this idyllic setting to cultivate pearls from Japanese pearl oysters. The tight security at the 1153-hectare sea farm at Bohey Dulang and the difficult access to the other Semporna islands have inadvertently helped to preserve the diverse marine life in the area. A dive into the clear water here is an experience: fanciful coral formations and colourful, boggle-eyed fish in an awesome underwater landscape of cliffs and valleys.

Truly Semporna island can be proud of soft sand, clear seas, rich marine life and intriguing lagoons.

The only island frequently visited by picnickers and swimmers is Pulau Sibuan. Otherwise, only small groups of Bajaus use the islands, living much the way they have for the last hundred years. There are now plans to declare these islands as a national marine park to protect the diverse lifeforms especially the corals which are as varied as those of the Great Barrier Reef.

Pulau Sipadan deserves special mention as Sabah's only true oceanic island. Lying 30 kilometres offshore, the island is less than a 1.6 kilometres in circumference. This rocky outcrop was once a sanctuary for Nicobar pigeons. Today, the island is frequented by green turtles which lay their eggs on its soft sand. There are some recommendations to turn the island into a marine reserve. Within less than 50 feet from the shore line the water plunges from five or ten feet deep straight down to 2,000 feet. It houses the best marine life in Malaysia and one of the best in the world. Visiting divers have often exclaimed that they have dived in the Maldives (now popular world wide for diving enthusiasts) the Red Sea, the Barrier Reef but never have they seen so much in one place as Pulau Sipadan. A local company, Borneo Divers, runs regular trips to Sipadan now.

Back on the mainland the Danum Valley, part of the Sabah Foundation forest concession areas, has now been preserved as reserve for scientific study. It is perhaps the best remaining untouched area of lowland rain forest certainly in Borneo and possibly in South East Asia.

Over the Tawau Hills amidst cocoa and oil palm plantations is a park declared in 1979 to protect the watershed supplying water to Tawau town. Lowland and hill forest surround volcanic outcrops over the 27,972-hectare park which has already lost two-thirds of its original cover to logging.

A four-hour walk from the park entrance leads to a hot spring. But just a few minutes from that entrance is a cool, green spot of a clear waterfall with a deep natural pool at its foot. Hornbills can be heard honking from the jungle depths. Other animals shy away from people and are seldom seen.

Like these animals, the park, islands and other natural aspects of the Tawau Division are also rarely seen. Access to the region by road can be rough, and although the towns are also connected by air, few people see this part of Sabah. The following pages captures many of these scenic sports, giving you a glimpse of another world even as you relax in your chair.

125 (following page) Tawau is an important service centre for agricultural and timber products. As Sabah's third largest port town, roads and a domestic air service link it and its rich hinterland with the rest of the state. The Tawau division was created as more and more settlements opened up on the east coast. In 1936, it was fused with Sandakan, only to be re-established in 1954. New wharves and warehouses were built to help mind the increasing flow of cocoa and oil palm from the division. Container facilities were subsequently added to the port. Today, more timber passes through Tawau than Sandakan, whose shadow it grew up in. The one-time village of two hundred is now home to a mix of Chinese, Bajaus, Malays and other ethnic groups totalling 60,000.

126   128
127

126 A bird's-eye view of a tropical rain forest in Tawau. In recent years Tawau has wrested the title 'Timber town' from Sandakan. Aggressive reaforestation has created Sabah's largest man-made timber forests at Tawau, Sabah Softwoods Plantation. Among the trees planted here is a fast growing species known as *Albizia Falcataria*, which can grow to an amazing 30.5 metres in 64 months, a fact acknowledged by the Guinness Book of Record.

127 Hands big and small ensure that cocoa gets harvested. The crop is grown on big plantations and smallholdings where children develop an intimacy with their state's major export crop at an early age. Fieldwork means collecting and splitting the pods by hand and scooping moist fresh beans into baskets, bound for fermenting and drying at the factories. Processed beans are sold worldwide but some are sent to the cocoa factory at Tawau where they are turned into cocoa butter and powder for foreign markets.

128 Logs are "herded" neatly down the Kalabakan river by boats on the way to the harbour for export. In a land as formidably forested and hilly as Sabah, rivers haves become important as paths to the interior and new settlements as well as fishing grounds and a route to timber troves. The Kalabakan River flows through prime timber country that has since shed its jungle mantle for a fast-growing man-made forests with trees that mature in 64 months.

129 Lahad Datu, fondly referred to as Sabah's cowboy town, does have frontier ambience. Bajau water villages still hug the coast as they have for a hundred years and native boats still call with their hauls of fish from Darvel Bay. The lifeline of the town is tied to timber, cocoa and oil palm like other towns along Tawau's coast. Small as it is, the people are a varied lot – Chinese, Sulus, Bajaus, Idahans with Indonesians and Filipinos drawn by the development of the land. They are part of a recent migrant wave that include the Cocos Islanders from coral islands south-west of Java. About 3,000 of them now live between Lahad Datu and Tawau, working in cocoa, oil palm and rubber estates. They have kept their culture alive though tinged by the influences of a Scottish family who moved from Indonesia to the Cocos Islands to work on coconut plantations.

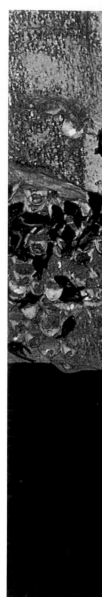

130 131

130 The Madai limestone massif, lying midway between Lahad Datu and Tawau, is clearly visible for about 30km. The massif rises about 250 metres from the forest floor. Harvesting of birds' nest here is a hereditary right of the Idahan people. The two major groups of animals that make the caves their home are the birds and the bats. The swiftlets are out foraging during the day and only return to roost at night. The bats, on the other hand, sleep during the day and search for food at night.

131 Clustered on rocky ceilings, cave swiftlets are remarkably adept at finding their way to their own nests. The brown rumped swiftlet is one of the cave-dwellers that breed in the Gomantong Caves near Sandakan. The swiftlet's white nests are Sabah's prized delicacy. Its first nest is thick and tinted with blood, the second nest – which is the most valuable – is whiter and thinner while the third is small, thin and stained with blood. The nests are built of gummy secretions from the birds' salivary glands that usually bind plant matter and feathers. A few swiftlets build their nests almost purely out of saliva and these are the nests the Chinese are willing to pay high prices for.

132   133

132 Semporna's markets are found on the wooden jetty where fresh fish are sold together with jungle and farm produce.

133 Semporna is relatively small and isolated town off Sabah's south-eastern coast and can be reached by air, road and sea. The town is built on an old coral reef believed to be 35,000 years old and whose exposure is caused by a general uplift of the land and surrounding sea bed. The land and seascape has not remained static over recent geological time and evidence of change is revealed by the presence of raised reefs in certain areas.

134 Pulau Omadal

135 A traditional sapit lies near completion under a coconut grove. The elaborate details that adorn the boat are rare these days as interest in local craftsmanship declines. Basic boat-building skills are essential in the coastal areas though, where a variety of native boat styles still live on.

136 Umakil bin Bararuddin is a Bajau wood-carver on Pulau Bum Bum who wields his skill for burial posts. His intense concentration belies the fact that he is in his 70s.

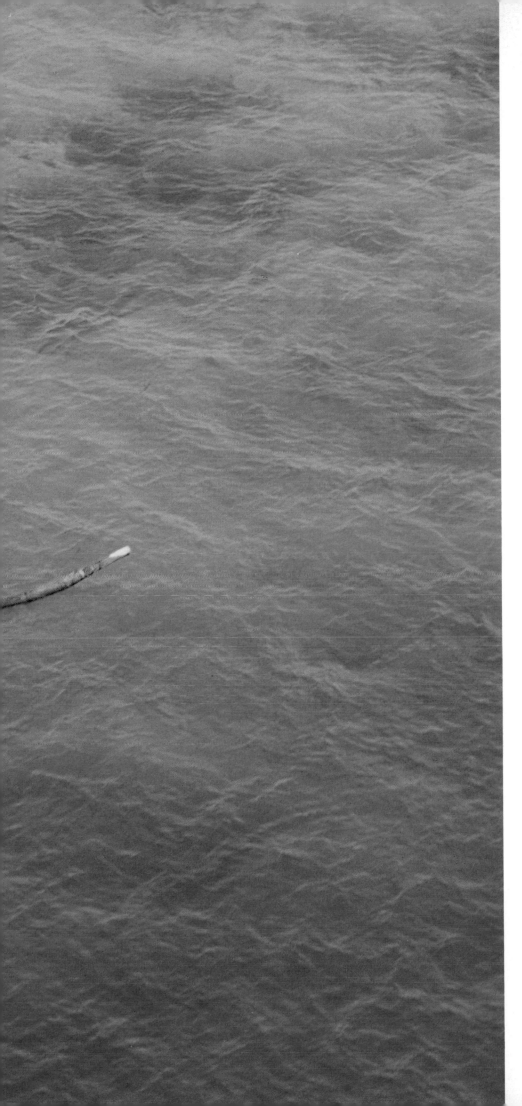

137 Temptingly blue, the sea seduces two Bajau Laut (Sea Bajau) fishermen on a *dapang* (fishing boat) to hunt its waters. Basic methods such as nets and handlines and sometimes illicit home-made bombs are used by the local fishermen.

138 *(following page)* Emerald sea surround a Bajau maritime village. Their attap and stilts homes surprisingly could stand up well to tropical storms and waves. Wooden plankways link each home and every family has at least a fishing boat or *dapang* in the 'front yard'.

139 *(previous page)* Until the turn of the century, many of the Bajaus spent their life in boats on the sea. According to a legend, the Bajau were once engaged to escort the daughter of the Sultan of Johor to Sulu to marry the Sultan. However, they were attacked by Brunei pirates and lost the bride. Not wishing to return to Johor, they decided to roam the seas. Thus, they became known as the Sea Gypsies. The Bajaus on the West Coast have now settled down on the land and farm for a living. However, many of them still live in boats and lead a nomadic life.

140 Pulau Bodgaya (left) and Pulau Bohey Dulang are volcanic islands which consist of high peaks of exposed volcanic rock rising well over 450 metres above the sea. They represent the northern rim of a now flooded volcanic caldeira. The rim is completely submerged in the south.

141 A jewel of an island breeds gems for sale on land. The Kaya Pearl Company operates a pearl farm over the sheltered sea where one can just make out racks of Japanese pearl oysters afloat.

140   141

143   146

144

145

142 *(previous page)* Pulau Mantabuan is a low island of raised coral limestone with volcanic rock base beneath. In the background are Pulau Bohey Dulang (left) and Pulau Bodgaya.

143 Millepora are hard corals common along the reef rims and upper slopes, especially at sheltered or semi-exposed sites. These branching corals with hard, spiky bodies provide shelter for fish and a variety of invertebrates.

144 Sea whips — pencil thin corals — wind entwined across a dark, soft sea studded by stars of minute marine life sparkling in flashlight.

145 Individual animals team up instinctively to form the convoluted ridges characteristic of brain coral.

146 Table corals spread out flat and wide. Some grow over a metre in diameter and are good hiding places for small fish.

147 Pulau Mabul provides the villagers with coconut trees which they use to build their homes supplemented with nipah palm from the mainland. Agriculture and fishing make up much of their very self-sufficient lifestyle.

148 Polyps on the sea fans.

149 Unafraid of divers, a parrot fish proudly displays its vivid colours for a portrait.

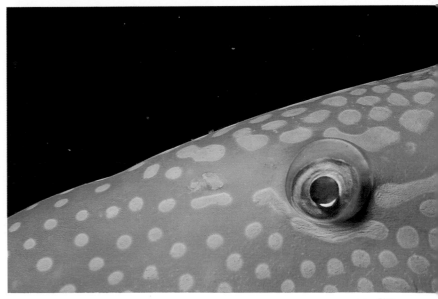

150 Bajau children bunch up for a picture at their wooden sea house. Beyond their traditional stilt village, the twentieth century lies gleaming enticingly on the shores of the mainland, perhaps luring them to a new life.

151 Pulau Danawan is one of many island with a native population, this one being a Suluk community, living in tradition amidst a sea of change.

152 *(following page)* Lying about 15 to 20 kilometres off Semporna peninsula is a chain of reefs and small islands which constitute the only barrier reefs of any size off Sabah's coast. Pulau Sipadan lies about 10 kilometres south of the barrier and is the only oceanic island in Sabah's waters. The island is low and flat and rises abruptly from about 600 metres. Its most interesting and impartial features lie underwater. The shallow reef which marks the upper edge of the seamount is exceptionally luxuriant and immediately below it are vertical cliffs, ledges, underhangs, caverns, steep slopes and ridges. The water here which has horizontal visibility of 30 metres is rich in marine life with unusual species of sort coral and numerous seafans and fish which are rarely seen elsewhere in Sabah.

150   151

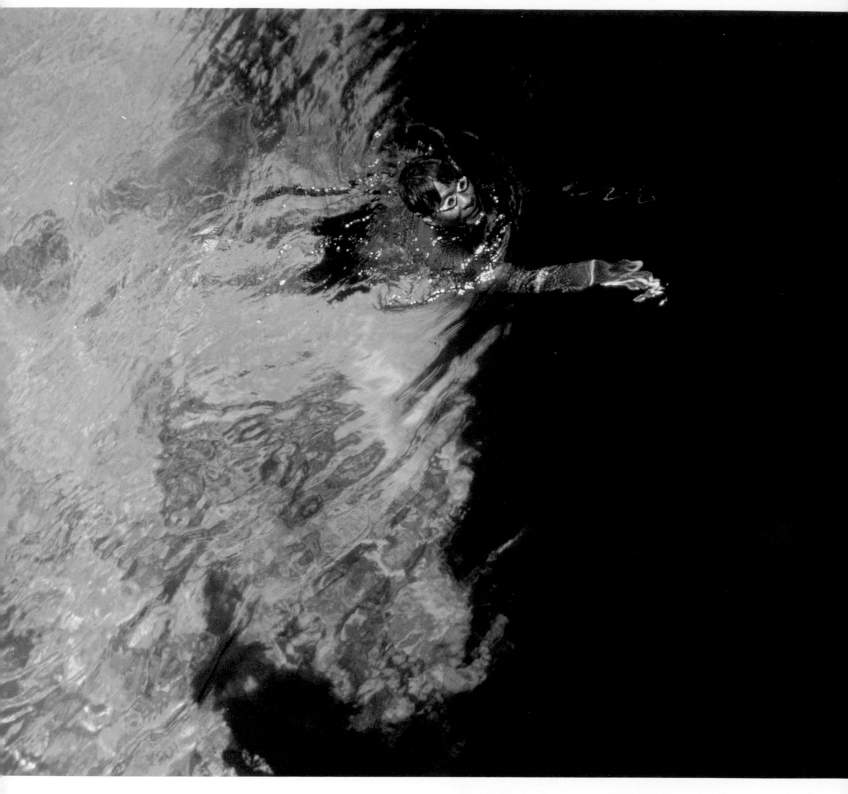

153 A Bajau boy enjoying himself in the sea off Pulau Sipadan. The sudden steep drop of the beach is marked by darkish water.

154 Sea whips are soft corals, usually red but sometimes blue or white too.

155 This flamboyant citizen of the reefs is known by many names. Lion fish and dragon fish are familiar tags. Pretty as it may be, its design is meant as a warning to would-be predators. Its spines are tipped with a poison so strong, a sting from a 12cm fish can inflict severe pain on a person.

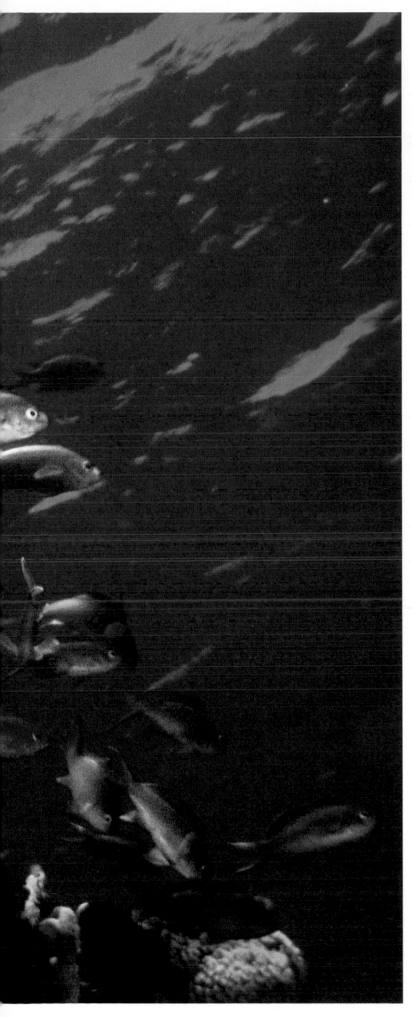

156 The most interesting feature of Pulau Sipadan is its fish fauna. On the shallow reef rims lies a variety of coral associated fish life that is rich and diverse. Some are red, others yellow or purple.

157 The large robber or coconut crab *(Birgus latro)* is a common invertebrate fauna on Pulau Sipadan. They are voracious and robust scavengers that live on the strand vegetation.

158 A guitar fish glides silently and shark-like through light-dappled waters.

156   157

  158

159 A diver's flash light picks up the innumerable polyps that make up a sea fan.

160 Soft coral.

161 At 15 metres below the waters of Pulau Sipadan, the underwater world is dull green and blue. But an underwater torch reveals its true hues. Soft corals like these effuse with strong red and dainty white.

162 Green turtles *(Chelonia Mydas)* are common sight in waters off Pulau Sipadan. They come to the shores of this uninhabited island to lay their eggs.

159   161   162

160

Chapter Six

THE INTERIOR DIVISION

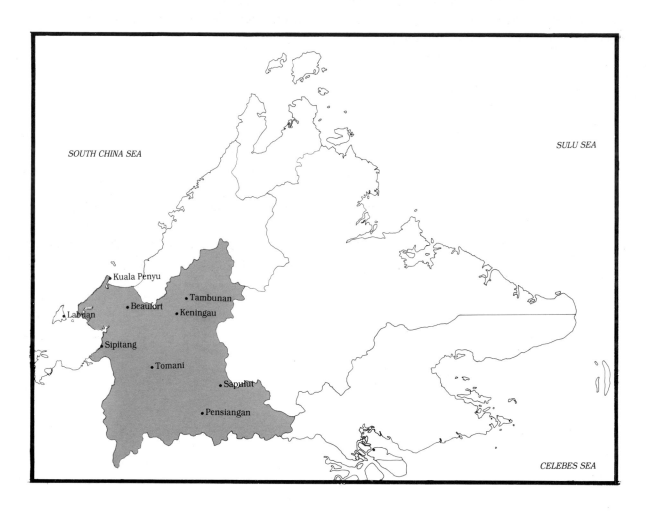

The name "Interior" instantly conjures up an untamed, jungle frontier. But Sabah's Interior Division has begun shedding that image. Following Man's progress over the past century, the jungles in this division in some areas have given way to plantations and paddy fields, while areas such as Gunung Lotong district which crosses to the Sandakan and Tawau divisions has hardly been explored. Roads have been built over hills and valleys linking villages and towns. And here the only passenger rail service in all of Borneo clatters through wild country.

Despite its rapid progress, the Interior has not lost all its frontier spirit. Locked between the Crocker Range and the borders of Indonesian Kalimantan, the land is still mountainous, jungly and difficult to cross.

But the journey to Keningau town, the administrative heart of the Interior, is a fine one. A tarred road meanders its way over the Crocker Range from the state capital of

Kota Kinabalu past the pastoral district of Tambunan before it reaches the Keningau plains.

The drive is breathtaking for bordering the road are some of Sabah's most beautiful countryside. Paddy fields dotted with buffaloes give way to terraced farmland cut into foothills while pineapple fields cling to steep slopes, rising with the hills.

The air grows cleaner and cooler as the road climbs up the contours of the Crocker Range. Wooden makeshift stalls tempt drivers to stop for sweet pineapples. The green hills are crowned by little houses with montane forests creeping into the cool slopes. Along the way, there is always wall of earth on one shoulder and a drop into a valley on the other.

Round this bend is the jungle, round that bend, the distant sea. Round another the quilted valley plain of Tambunan lies stretched out. Tambunan is Kadazan or

Dusun country where 17,000 people grow mainly wet paddy and some vegetables.

Before Tambunan got its name and its fields, it was covered with lush rainforest and home only to wild animals. According to a local folklore, the valley was chanced upon by Gombunan, a warrior from the legendary but crowded Nunuk Ragang, where all Kadazan or Dusun come from. The valley was fertile and those who followed Gombunan subsequently settled there.

On the eastern side of the hills, the Tonsudong tribe eyed the industrious Kadazan or Dusun enviously. They launched a sudden attack on the newcomers but were driven back, cursing and vowing revenge. One day, the Tonsudongs spied Gombunan working alone in a field. A pack of them descended, overpowered him, hacked him to pieces and carried his head away in glee. His people mourned his death and named their new land after him as a tribute.

Soon after that came the Tamadon tribe to the Crocker Range slopes west of the valley. They were friendly people who helped the Gombunans when the Tonsudongs launched their next attack. The hostile Tonsudongs were beaten so badly, they never returned. To celebrate their victory, the people agreed to a union of their tribes. The valley was renamed Tambunan, a fusion of the names, Tamadon and Gombunan.

Today, more than 70 villages are sprinkled all over the valley's 1,295 square kilometres. Churches are also as scattered as the villages for three-quarters of the Kadazans or Dusuns here are Christians. Sundays mean both mass and *tamus*. A visitor may be gently distracted from the *tamu*'s hubbub by hymns sung in lilting Kadazans.

Further up the road is Sunsuron where there is a sizeable Muslim community. There is also a Muslim orphanage run by the Majlis Ugama Islam Sabah (MUIS) located here.

Solidly grounded in Tambunan is a memorial where one of Sabah's heroes, Mat Salleh, once had a fort. Mat Salleh had rebelled against Chartered Company rule. In return for a pardon for him and his men, he accepted the Company's offer to live in Tambunan, but he felt cheated when not all his men were pardoned and refused to sign the agreement. Tambunan was not under the company's control at that time and it had hoped that Mat Salleh would work with the company to help them control Tambunan. He refused by not signing the agreement and the skirmishes continued. The "rebellion" finally come to a halt here when in 1900, on January 31st Mat Salleh was killed by a stray bullet.

The annual Harvest Festival celebrations are a very special event for the Kadazan or Dusun and their kindred peoples. According to a local folklore, in the beginning were *Kinoingan*, the Kadazan or Dusun god, his wife, *Suminundu,* and their only daughter *Huminodun.* When *Kinoingan* created the Kadazans or Dusuns, he sacrificed *Huminodun* to feed them. Bits of her body were planted like seeds and paddy, the people's staple food, grew from her. Because it sprang from *Huminodun*, the Kadazans believe paddy carries a spirit, the *Bambaazon.* Grateful for *Kinoingan's* gift, they honour the *Bambaazon* at their yearly festival so that the spirit will bless their next harvest.

After Tambunan, the way to Keningau winds past Sabah's second highest peak, the 2,642-metre Mount Trus Madi, and moves into Murut territory. Keningau, Tenom and Pensiangan – the traditional Murut Lands – are hilly country and becaue of this, the Muruts are known as hill people.

The drive over the Crocker Range continues to be an unforgettable experience although much of the forests have been logged, forcing the lowland Nabai Muruts to rely more heavily on cultivation of hill paddy, yam, maize and sweet potato. Sugar cane is also grown together with fruits like bananas, durians and papayas. Some work in the rubber plantations, the timber industry and nearby towns.

The Keningau plains are no longer jungle but cultivated fields and scrubland created by logging. Reflecting the industry around it, Keningau town now has a number of hotels, office buildings and shophouses. The town attracts migrants workers like the Filipinos and Indonesians.

South of Keningau is Tenom. This small provincial town which is the terminus of Sabah's railway south out of Beaufort. Work on a railway system for Sabah began in 1896 at Weston on the west coast. It look almost ten years for the Chartered Company to lay 186 kilometres of tracks linking Jesselton to the districts of Putatan, Kinarut, Papar, Kimanis and Membakut and in the process opening up land for rubber cultivation.

During the war the railway was badly damaged but priority was given to its reconstruction under the Reconstruction and Development Plan 1946 to 50. Cargo and passenger trains still run to the interior from Kota Kinabalu.

In contrast to the bucolic views along the road into the Interior, the 49-km train ride plunges into rugged hills, rumbling through stone tunnels. It challenges the Padas River, running 238 metres below the tracks in the Padas Gorge, past frothing rapids. Despite the long ride, the journey is relatively comfortable compared to the ones taken by early settlers who had to hack through the territory with their knives and battle up rapids for access.

But the territory has its charm. The Muruts have always lived here. According to a legend told by the Timogon Muruts around Tenom, a great flood once inundated the world, drowning all but one man who escaped by climbing a magic coconut tree that grew taller as the waters rose. When the flood finally receded, the man climbed down. He found an old woman, stricken by an ugly skin disease. He failed to realize that she was an immortal and ran away in disgust when she suggested that they marry to return mankind to the world.

While he searched fruitlessly for his friends, she fashioned a clay doll shaped like her without disease. She spat red betel nut juice on it to bring the doll to life and then the old woman returned to heaven. The man came back and fell in love with the living doll and eventually married her believing that she was the women healed of her illness. They had many children and spread their kind all over the world

The tale also explains how death and diseases came to be Man's lot. A fool to choose the doll, the man's descendents were "destined" to be born of clay and to return to earth by death. If the man had married the old woman, his children would have been blessed by immortality.

But it was more than clay bodies and diseases that caused the Murut population to shrink sharply between 1915 and 1950.

The Rundum Rebellion of 1915, for instance, claimed the lives of hundreds of Murut men. Rundum lies in the deep south, beyond Tenom, and is difficult to reach even today. In their haste to reach the Interior, the Chartered Company forced the Muruts to build bridle-paths for ponies through the dense hills. Although they were given a wage, the Muruts were not used to salaried work. The British imposed taxes on tapioca, coconut trees and paddy which the natives use to make *tapai*, a fermented rice wine essential at every ceremony, happy or sad. Then came a tax on jungle clearing which affected the Murut practice of slashing and burning trees for farming land.

These moves by the Chartered Company threatened the core of Murut life. Many Iban government agents also preyed on the Muruts by demanding more taxes than those imposed and creating taxes where there were none.

The last straw came in 1914 when an eight-month drought destroyed much of the Murut crop. In desperation, the people revolted, led by the Murut chief, Antanum.

Antanum, like the earlier local hero Mat Salleh, was said to be blessed with supernatural powers. A dream showed him how to build his marvellous underground fort on a hillside. The fort had seven connected chambers shored up by wood and bamboo, and camouflaged by earth. Sharpened bamboo stakes and pits protected and booby-trapped the entire slope. The whole area was defended by about a thousand Muruts.

The climax came on March 6, 1915 when Rundum was burned by the British and many Muruts either wounded or killed. Martial law was declared and Antanum's fort came under siege on April 14. Three days of fighting followed before the Murut chief finally surrendered. The Muruts lost their best men. Starvation, drought and disease made the rout of the people complete. As a result, many Muruts died. Only 18,724 Muruts were recorded in the 1951 population census. Social and medical services were given to restore their numbers. Today, they number about 40,000 possibly matching their old population.

Muruts now enjoy a higher standard of living, education and contact with the outside world. These benefits, however, come at the cost of traditional ways, some fading, others evolving to match a changing environment. The Muruts' hunting skill with the blowpipe is fast losing out to the shotgun. Longhouses capable of boarding a whole village and built on land bounded by a river are being replaced by smaller, more individual homes at the water's edge.

As these longhouses vanish, so do the *lansaran* – a sunken, springy wooden platform. The *lansaran* is traditionally a central feature of Murut longhouses. Ritual and festive dances and singing are done with people bouncing and swaying on the trampoline-like *lansaran*. Even jumping contests are held.

During World War Two, Pensiangan in the far south was a waystation for Japanese troops moving across the country. When the war ended 6,000 Japanese soldiers surrendered at Pensiangan. They were made to trek to Beaufort across the hills. Murut retribution took its toll and many thousands were killed along the way. Some said the Muruts fell back on their headhunting ways.

Strange as it may seem, headhunting in Sabah and Sarawak was a way of gaining favour with the women, a way for ardent suitors to prove their manhood and love to their sweethearts. Heads were generally received with much whooping and celebration before they were preserved by drying or smoking.

Headhunting was regarded by Westerners as barbaric and the practice was eventually banned by the Chartered Company. The move was reinforced with Christianity and Islam which eventually instilled a new set of morals into the people.

As with the Kadazans or Dusuns, some Muruts have integrated Christianity with their animistic beliefs. Others have resisted conversion to it and Islam. Ritual specialists still exist with surviving animistic rituals.

And so, as Sabah pushes for progress with multi-million dollar plants for timber, pulp, paper and power, and a modern sports complex at Keningau, ancient incantations can be heard in the winds blowing over ancestral Murut lands.

163 Murut women in their traditional costumes.

164 *(previous page)* No more the provincial town it once used to be, Keningau, the capital of the Interior Residency, can now boast of up-to-date facilities like a modern sports stadium and a decent hotel. Around it, timber-based factories provide jobs for the people.

165

165 Neat rows of pepper plants cover the hill slopes at Apin Apin near Keningau. Primarily a smallholder's crop, pepper is one of Sabah's minor agricultural products.

166 Some of the finest tobacco was grown in Sabah at the end of the 19th century. Now that little tobacco grown is mainly for local use. Tobacco leaves are cured in drying sheds like one in the background.

167 Bent under the weight of her corn-filled *wakid* (bamboo basket), a Murut lady goes about the daily chore of moving her crop from the field to a stall for sale.

166   167

168 An aerial view looking north over Tambunan Valley. The name Tambunan is ac tually coined from the words 'Tam' and 'Bunan' after two groups of people – Tamadon and Gambunan – to mark their victory over their common enemy, the Tonsudung tribe. The 17,000 inhabitants here – almost all of whom are of Dusun/Kadazan origin – are mainly paddy farmers.

169 *(following page)* An aerial view looking south over Tambunan Valley. Tambunan is a sun-filled valley lying snug between the Crocker Range on the west and the Trus Madi on the east. Most of the valley dwellers are Christians but of late, inroads made by Islam have raised eye-catching golden-domed mos-ques across the valley. Progress here means a few more new shops and office blocks and a growing network of roads. The Kota Kinabalu-Keningau highway runs the length of the valley but the closeness it brings Tambunan with the outside world also draws young people away, enticed by the numerous job opportunities in the cities.

170 Women rather than men play significant roles in traditional rituals among the Kadazan and Murut people. Revered priestesses usually pass their knowledge down to young girls, usually their daughters. The rituals are heading for a slow death, bypassed by an educated generation generally satisfied with glimpses of the rituals at the annual Harvest Festival celebrations.

171 Head-dress of Penampang Kadazan is called *Siga Bobhizan.* Full ceremonial regalia bedecks a *bobohizan,* a Kadazan priestess, as she leads the *Magavau* rituals.

172 Swathed in traditional black and gold, Kadazan devotees. dance and chant at the *Magavau* rites performed at the annual Harvest Festival.

170 171
172

173 The Kadazan year begins with the paddy-planting season around June or July. Planting seedlings is backbreaking work in muddy waters restrained by brown bunds. The only comfort is a hat to keep the sun at bay. The paddy fields are never far from the family home or barn, which sometimes sits in the middle of the land. The Kadazans in Tambunan have long abandoned their longhouses for individual homes but houses are still built of wood, bamboo and thatch. A growing affluence is changing this, replacing thatch with tiles or zinc.

174 Buffaloes are as much a part of Tambunan's landscape as the terraced paddy fields. Besides their value as wealth, meat and help in ploughing, grazing herds keep the villages neat by cropping grass to a respectable level.

175 *(following page)* An aerial view of the terraced landscape of Tambunan.

173
174

176 While waiting for customers at a Sunday *tamu* in Tambunan, this Kadazan lady decides to take a puff.

177 Kadazans leaving the church after Sunday morning worship in Tambunan. The church was called St. Johns when it was first built in 1948. It was reconstructed in 1963 and it is now known as the Holly Cross.

176   177

178 Sunsuron, a *kampung* situated at the end of the Tambunan Valley is well-known for its rice terraces. It has a sizeable Muslim community and it also has a Muslim orphanage run by the Majlis Ugama Islam (MUIS).

179 The traditional bamboo basket or *wakid* is used by many of the ethnic groups in Sabah to carry their jungle or farm produce to the market place to trade. Seen here are two Kadazans or Dusuns women with their empty *wakids* on their backs returning home after a good day at the market.

178 179

180 Old world charm survives in rural Tenom as in this railway station. An experimental garden was located close to Tenom in 1899 which later became an agricultural research station. Some of the first rubber trees in Sabah were planted here. Tenom is also the terminus for Borneo's only passenger railway.

181 The Padas River has carved a heart-shaped loop out of its course in the Tenom district. The river will eventually flow straight past the tip of the "heart" and leave the ring of water behind in the landscape like a giant valentine.

180   181

182

182 A traditional Murut wedding ceremony in progress. The wedding is usually accompanied by drinking of *tapai* (rice of tapioca wine) and feasting.

183

183 Manicured park ground becomes the stage for a Timogon Murut dance accompanied by traditional gong music. Sabah's indigenous people have a wealth of dances which are performed with skill and dexterity. The movements reflect a cultural heritage and sometimes a religious significance. Both Muruts and Bajaus are known for a dance called the *Menggunatip*, Kadazans for *Sumazau*, Suluks for the *Daling-Daling*, and the Bajaus for the *Limbai*.

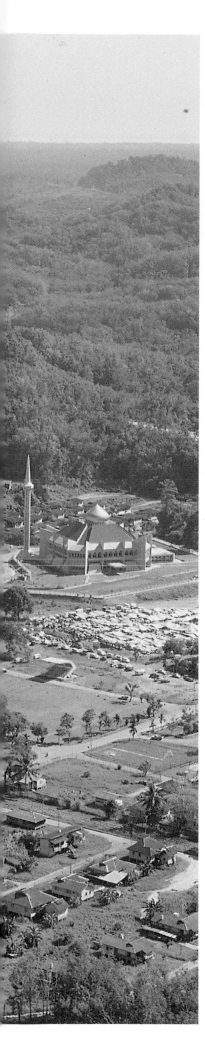

184 Beaufort is a small but modern riverine town on the lower stretches of the Padas River. It takes its name from L.P Beaufort, the Governor of Labuan and British North Borneo from 1895 to 1900. Around the turn of the century, tobacco followed by rubber became important crops of the Beaufort area. The older section of the town is built high on stilts.

185 Two adventurers rafting down the Padas River as a train rushes by.

184   185

186   187

186 A state-wide festival brings out Sabah's indigenous costumes. Except for a tell-tale watch, the traditional hairstyle and dress characteristic of the Lundayeh could well be a scene from days long gone. The Lundayeh people were originally classified as part of the Murut group. In Sarawak, they are still so classified and are known as Lundayeh, Lunbawang and various other names. However, linguistically it has now been shown that theirs is not of the Murutic family and in Sabah they are classified separately. They live in the area around the Sabah-Sarawak-Kalimantan borders. A Lundayeh pipe band (bamboo flute) is a pleasure to the ears.

187 Kuala Penyu, originally a small fishing village whose population has increased tremendously over the past 20 years. Oil palm schemes have been introduced into the area. The population comprises Kadazans, Bajaus, Bisayas Kedayans, Chinese and others.

188 Pensiangan has always been one of the more remote Murut districts. The first District Officer was posted to Pensiangan in early 1915 and Pensiangan continued to be a centre for administration until 1974 when the District Office was moved to Nabawan for logistical reasons. Even today Pensiangan can only be reached by perahu (native longboat) or helicopter. The first logging road is expected here soon.

189 A Murut man mends his fishing nets in a longhouse at Kampong Silungoi in Pensiangan. The Muruts are hill people and were once feared headhunters. They live in longhouses and hunt with blowpipes and spears. Besides hunting, they also gather jungle produce such as rattan and resin as well as planting paddy on shifting cultivation basis for their livelihood. Old tribal names such as Timogun, Tagol, Nabong, etc are still used to refer to different Murut groups.

190 *(following page)* Long Pa Sia is a tiny, rustic border village near Kalimantan. It is the centre of the area inhabited by the Lundayeh people and sits 1,100 metres above sea level. Its proximity to Kalimantan makes it a convenient stop for people crossing the borders.

191 Barely influenced by the modern world, residents of Long Pa Sia make their way through life which has hardly changed over the years, like crossing over suspended bamboo bridges loaded with produce from their farms.

192 Long Pa Sia immigration office.

193 The Malaysian Airline System (MAS) connects rural towns like Long Pa Sia with a domestic service. A small plane uses the grass runway once a week. Beneath a signpost declaring the field an airstrip, villagers get a ringside seat to the aerial event.

192

191   193

Chapter Seven

LABUAN

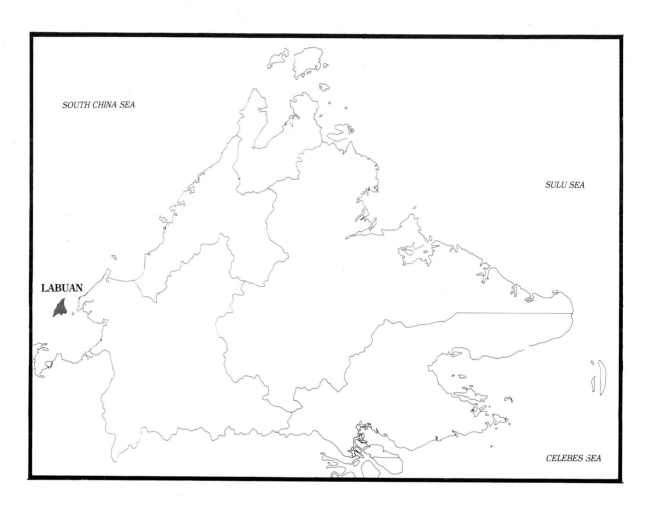

Labuan was uninhabited and desolate when Brunei ceded the tiny 90-square kilometre island to the British in the middle of the nineteenth century. Only fishermen used the island as a resting place during their rounds. However, they were not interested in its fine harbour, strategic location and coal deposits.

But the British were. Labuan was where the East India Company officials fled from their trading post on Balambangan Island when it was attacked by pirates. The British were thankful for the low-lying forested island, its fresh water and good climate after the barren conditions of Balambangan.

When coal was found in 1845, the British pressed even harder for possession of the island. Coal meant that Labuan could become a refuelling stop for British steamships. Ships meant trade and this was what they wanted to develop in the South China Sea.

Labuan came to the British as a Christmas present on December 24, 1846. James Brooke, then trying to establish his position in Sarawak, became the island's first Governor. It was Britain's smallest colony even with the surrounding islands of Rusukan Besar, Rusukan Kecil, Keraman, Burong, Papar and Daat.

With the little colony came big hopes. Besides the trade potential, the British intended to check piracy with their navy from the new harbour at Victoria.

To encourage trade, Labuan was made a free port in 1848, but plans were foiled by a few unforeseen hitches. Native traders from Sulu and north-east Borneo were not interested in using Labuan as a market for their edible birds' nest and seed pearls. Trade was diverted from Labuan in 1873 when a German named Willie Shuck set up a small trading post in Sandakan Bay. Furthermore, other traders were selling their opium and tobacco far cheaper than their Labuan counterparts. And while coal was mined in the north of Labuan, it was inefficiently done and sold expensively.

Labour to work its coal mine was a problem, and to alleviate it James Brooke in 1850 started importing convict labour from Hong Kong to cut mining costs. They were also asked to clear jungle, build roads and work in the harbour. The move generated fears that Labuan might become a penal settlement. It never did, but riots and strikes over poor working conditions finally forced coal production to a halt in 1911.

While trade limped along with coal production, the Chinese were busy making Labuan their home. They started arriving in 1847, when Labuan opened its doors to settlers. They set up shops, selling mainly provisions, while some started growing vegetables and fruits like mango, mangosteen and pineapples. They also grew the first pepper in Labuan. Cash crops like coconut, sago and betelnut were not ignored either.

People who came to Labuan included the Kadazan or Dusun some of whom were once slaves and who escaped to Labuan because slavery was illegal on the island after the British took control. Malays sailed in from Brunei and craftsmen fashioned silver and brassware for sale. The Ibans made a brief appearance to sift through the island's jungles for bees' wax and camphor, which were exported to Singapore.

By 1890, Labuan was added to the British North Borneo Company's responsibilities together with mainland Sabah. For a while, coal mining was better managed and a railway line was laid to carry it from the mines to the harbour and trade began to pick up.

The colony became part of the Straits Settlement in 1907 and enjoyed many years of flourishing trade till the Japanese invaded on New Year's Day in 1942. Explosives rained on Labuan from air and sea.

When the dust settled and the war was over Labuan was conveniently added to Sabah's territory to become a Crown Colony after the war and looked towards rehabilitation. The island's free port status was reinstated on September 1, 1956 to revive its trade appeal.

The discovery of oil about 48 kilometres off Labuan in 1973 drastically reshaped the island's trade patterns. Sabah's only crude oil terminus stands at Labuan today, storing and handling crude oil from the offshore oilfields.

Labuan became a federal territory on April 16, 1984. It is now administered directly by the Federal Government.

194 Inexpensive anchorage in Labuan's waters tempts tankers to sit idle on the waves for years — long enough for an underwater garden to sprout on the ships' bottoms where fish graze askew on an upside-down field.

195 Victoria is Labuan's port and main town. Ferries shuttle people over the stretch of sea separating it from Menumbok and Sipitang on the mainland. The duty-free port attracts shoppers from Brunei and mainland Sabah. Visitors are also lured by its lovely beaches.

196 Neatly laid war graves at Labuan instil an illusion of peace over the violent end of 3,992 Allied War dead. Like a sentinel over their graves, the Cross of Sacrifice was unveiled on January 10, 1953, by Sir Ralph Hone, then Governor of British North Borneo. The tribute came eight years after the Australian Ninth Division's landing in Labuan.

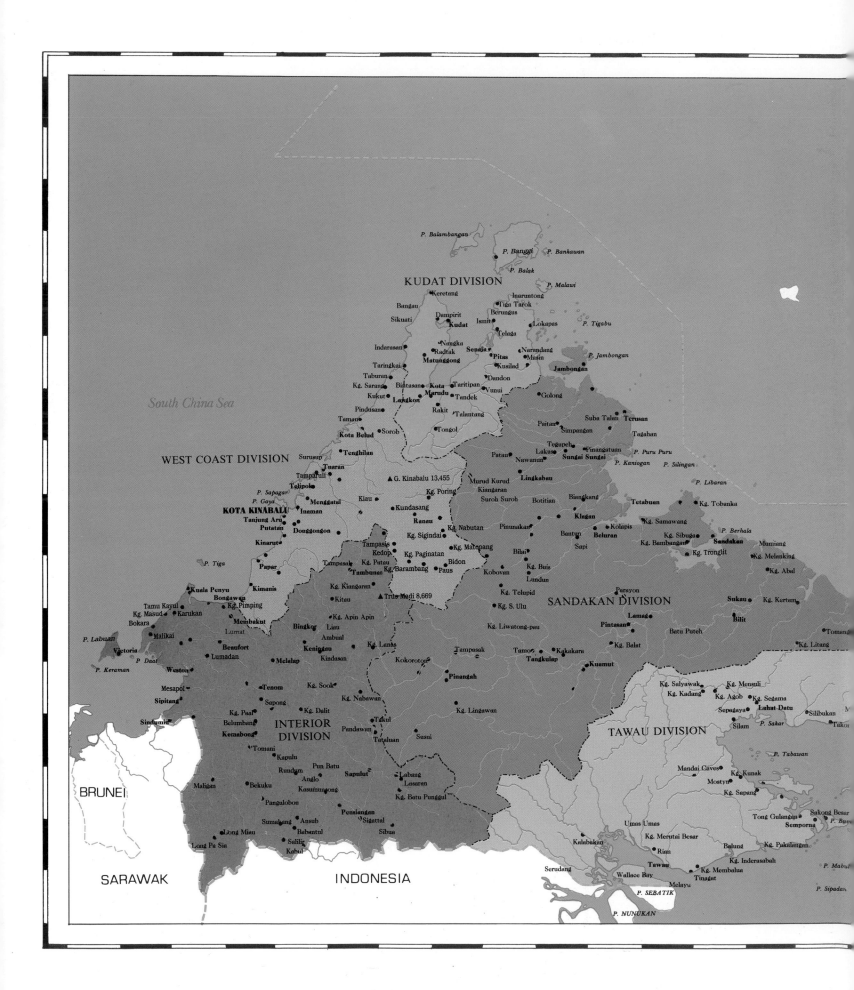

SABAH

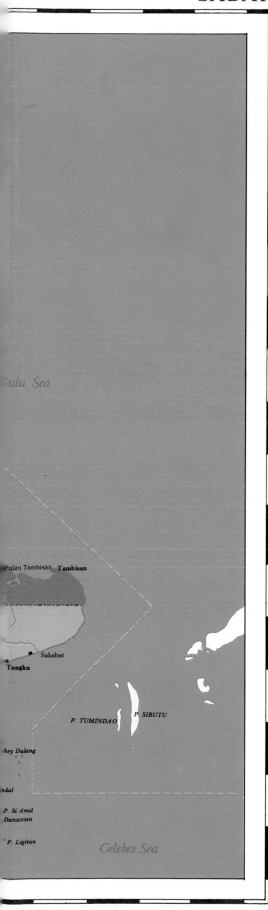

Sulu Sea

Pulau Tambisan　**Tambisan**

● Sahabat
Tungku

P. TUMINDAO　*P. SIBUTU*

hey Dulang

dal

P. Si Amil
Danawan

P. Ligitan

Celebes Sea

MALAYSIA

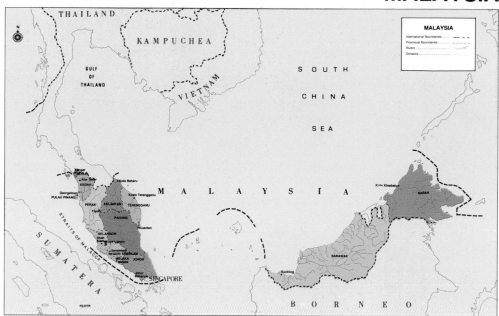

ACKNOWLEDGEMENTS

I would like to acknowledge my gratitude and thanks to my wife Vialyne and the following people who helped make the publication of this book possible: Datuk Joseph Pairin Kitingan, Yee Fong Chun, A.G. Sullivan, Tommy Chang, Krishnan S., Shamsuddin Mat Isa, Ahmad Kabber, Kim Lee, Ee Sim Teo-Machado and Allen Wan.

And my very special thanks to God for granting me life, strength, wisdom and encouragement to accomplish this project, for I know without his rich blessings, the publication of this book would be impossible.

To God be the glory for all that He has done.

Peter Chay
(Publisher, photographer)

PHOTO CREDITS

Tommy Chang	:	19, 21, 22, 23, 24, 25, 28, 30, 63, 64, 105, 107, 143, 144, 146, 148, 149, 150, 153, 154, 155, 156, 157, 158, 159, 160, 161, 162, 171, 172, 185.
Sabah Museum	:	44, 55, 97, 124, 130, 135, 136, 163, 182, 186, 189.
Sabah Parks	:	35, 36, 61, 62, 65, 112.
Nicholas Johnston	:	29, 145.
R. Stucbing	:	39, 111.
S. Sreedharan	:	102, 113, 114, 115, 116, 118.
Victor Wah	:	99, 127.
WWF/C.M. Francis	:	131.
Hasbullah Latiff	:	48, 56, 57, 183.
MAS	:	53, 54, 191, 193.